Diary of an Accidental Dad

Alex Goetchius

Martin Sisters Publishing

Published by

Martin Sisters Books, a division of Martin Sisters Publishing, LLC

www.martinsisterspublishing.com

Copyright © 2012 by Alex Goetchius

The unauthorized reproduction or distribution of this copyrighted work is illegal. Criminal copyright infringement, including infringement without monetary gain, is investigated by the Federal Bureau of Investigation and is punishable by up to 5 (five) years in federal prison and a fine of $250,000.

No part of this book may be reproduced or transmitted in any form or by any means, electronic or mechanical, including photocopying, recording, or by any information storage and retrieval system, without permission in writing from the publisher.

All rights reserved. Published in the United States by Martin Sisters Books, an imprint of Martin Sisters Publishing, LLC, Kentucky.

ISBN: 978-1-937273-41-5

Memoir

Editor: Kathleen Papajohn
Illustration on title page by: Lukas Netelkos Goetchius

Printed in the United States of America
Martin Sisters Publishing, LLC

Dedication

Dedicated to Nicole, Lukas and Noelle who fill my head with more wild ideas, my journals with more stories, and my heart with more love than a simple man like me deserves.

an imprint of Martin Sisters Publishing, LLC

Foreword By John Colangelo

Ever tell a story about your Family or kids and get a bewildered look from your audience? Then you say, "I guess you had to be there." Well Accidental Dad IS there. These stories hit so close to home that they have to be true, but they are written in a witty, articulate, self-deprecating style that keeps me looking for the next installment with anticipation.

Dad's struggles to find a place in childhood society for a hyper-kinetic but brilliant son are both hysterical and endearing. The fine line between being over-indulgent, protective, free-wheeling and disciplinarian are crossed, stomped and drawn again over and over with the inner dialog we all have with ourselves of "please don't let me fuck up my kids" ringing in his head.

Accidental Dad writes for the unsung Dads with shirts with missing buttons and the soccer Moms that pay for gymnastic lessons instead of getting their hair done. This is great writing on a subject you rarely see great writing on. Accidental Dad manages to capture our hearts, make us love his Family as much as he so clearly does, without being saccharine or preachy.

This is Erma Bombeck if she liked a good spanking and drank a bit too much. I can't wait until his little pixie of a daughter starts talking more.

my Daughter fell asleep in my arms last night

#1

My daughter fell asleep in my arms last night. It was the first time that's ever happened. She rested her cheek on my shoulder and her little hand wrapped itself around my finger. I was so moved by how precious and forever this moment was, a tear spilled from my eye, ran down my cheek and dripped from my neck onto her face. She stirred for just a second but then fell back to sleep.

For the entirety of her life my daughter has fallen asleep sucking on a plump and nourishing bosom. The comfort in a suckled breast is more intoxicating than any other "high" God's green earth can offer, so it's no wonder some kids have a hard time giving it up. I myself have been known to fall asleep with a boob in my mouth from time to time, and I can tell you first hand, it's a hard habit to break.

My daughter fell asleep in my arms last night. I sang to her in a deep low whisper that hummed through her body as I rocked her in my arms. With each note, my breath tickled her skin and the warm breeze lulled her deeper into sleep. Her body collapsed completely into my arms and she began to snore softly. I waited for a little puddle of drool to drip from the corner of her mouth and pool up on my shoulder, before I took her upstairs to bed.

The last words of my song trailed off and she fell into a quiet slumber as I lowered her slowly into her crib. I knew it wouldn't take much to wake her up. One errant toe or finger that grazed the wooden gate of the crib, or one soft scrape of her skin against the scruff of my unshaven face, would wake her. And when she's woken from a sleep that deep, the only thing that will console her is "MOMMY!"

"FUCK!!! She's awake!!!"

My heart began to race and sweat beaded up on my flushed forehead. I looked down at her as she tried to reposition her restless body. Her ferocious "over tired cry" thundered in the distance. My insides churned with panic but my hands amazingly remained steady. My daughter laid on her belly and tucked her legs beneath her. I patted her back and covered her with a soft warm blanket. She fell back to sleep and into a delicious dream filled with princesses and cupcakes.

It feels really cool and truly amazing to connect with her in this way. It's so heartwarming and profound to have your kid feels so comfortable and safe in your arms, they willingly succumb to sleep's powerful pull.

I know there will be nights when my soft pats on her back, and the gentle touch of my fingers to her face won't be enough to put her back to sleep. Hopefully then she'll still find some comfort cradled in my arms and half asleep on my shoulder, even as she's screams at the top of her lungs, "MOM!!!"

ALEX GOETCHIUS

My Dad Says you're an asshole

#2

"My dad says you're an asshole!" Yup, I did say that, but I didn't think anyone was listening. I certainly didn't think anyone would repeat it. But that's what happened the day of my son's kindergarten graduation.

First off, let me just say something about kindergarten graduations. I know it's in vogue to trash ceremonies that celebrate mediocrity and striving for less. In essence, kindergarten graduation is nothing more than a celebration of moving past the second lowest rung on the education ladder. That said, my son's kindergarten experience was at times a war filled with angst, alienation and heartbreak. So to me, his survival was worthy of the finest of celebrations.

I've long ago realized anything more than a healthy dose of cynicism will turn your body's water molecules into sludge. So rather than question the validity of celebrating yet another over rated pop singer's Grammy, or a football team I have no connection to winning the Super Bowl, I just sit back and crack open a cold one. Life is too short not to celebrate all it has to offer.

One battle my son waged all year was a friend who played him like a bi-polar accordionist. At times the music was sweet, like the kind you might be serenaded with at a French or Italian restaurant. At other times the music was dissonant carnival music, egging on the circus clowns and burlesque stooges to finally get their revenge.

All my son wanted was for this kid to like him and he would have done almost anything to make that happen. And this asshole of a friend knew it, and made my son do parlor tricks for his friendship. "If you don't do this, I won't be your friend anymore" he used to tell my son. "If you do that, I'll be your best friend" he'd tease him with.

It killed me to watch my son work so hard for this kid's approval, when I knew he'd never be my son's best friend. After watching my son's heart get broken every other day, I finally told that to him, along with the now infamous "that kid's an asshole."

We were on my bike pedaling into town and then down to the beach. My son was sitting in a bike seat mounted to the handle bars of my bicycle. Having him in front of me and just under my chin was so much cooler than having him sit in a seat behind me. For one thing we could talk and sing and brainstorm together. And for another, from back there all he would be able to see is the crack of my ass hanging out of my pants, and all the really cool action after it's passed us by.

We'd talk about how our days went on those bike rides. We laughed about the fart that slipped out in his math class or the one that slipped out in one of my meetings at work. We vented about the thorns that that each of us experienced and we celebrated the roses each of us stopped long enough to smell.

More and more his stories revolved around this kid at school that were less like the sweet serenades and more like the twisted evil circus music. That's when I finally let those words slip from my lips. They came only a in a whisper, through a deep frustrated exhale. But my son's radar for expletives kicked in and he silently absorbed what I had to say.

I walked my son into school the day of his graduation while parents, grandparents and older siblings were congregated around the perimeter of the classroom and waiting for the ceremonies to commence. He pulled me over to his on again, off again best friend and mortal enemy. He looked into my eyes and said, "Tell him dad. Tell him." Then before I could ask what it was he wanted me to say, my son looked at this kid with wild eyes and pointed back at me and said for all to hear, "My dad says you're an asshole!"

I don't remember much after that other than pulling my son out of his class by the scruff of his neck, tossing him in the car, and peeling out of the parking lot, kicking up gravel and dust. I couldn't get out of there fast enough. We celebrated my son's graduation without his grandparents who were pissed off at having to come all that way for nothing, and without his pretend friend for once, not having the last say.

It's only now that we can laugh about my infamous remark, and my son has gotten over his long lost pretend friend. Through the course of all of that, I learned two valuable lessons. The first is that every heart-break is a lesson well learned. The lessons that we feel the most are the ones we remember best. And second, if you're going to whisper something on your bike that you don't want your kid to hear, make sure he's riding behind you, staring at the crack of your ass.

Penis Puppet

#3

My son was floating on his back in the bath last night. His body rested on the bottom of the tub and almost all of it was submerged. His hands were folded across his chest, his eyes were closed and a pleased look was painted on his face. He was making his wee Willie Johnson dance in the suds of the tub just as his little sister walked into the bathroom. She was fascinated by it bobbing in the water. It must have looked like a little alien with one eye open, poking its head thru white puffy clouds.

My son pulled from the bottom of the tub a rubber finger puppet of a six armed Buddha. He put it on young Master Johnson, and called out to my wife, "Hey mom, come and see my puppet show!" My daughter giggled with delight, and my wife called out over the noise of delirious children and running water, "DOES HE HAVE IT ON HIS FINGER!?" She expected him to be flipping me off with the puppet. I called back, "Yeah, his eleventh finger!"

Things I never thought I'd Be GOOD at

Recently I found myself in a situation where my daughter was a little cranky from hunger, and a little pissed off from having hot squishy poo in her diaper. If I had let either of those situations go on without attending to at least one of them, it would have been a disaster. Her screams which were loud enough to break glass would have blown out my ear drums, and her tears like pointy thorns would have poked out my eyes, if I had let that happen. But both situations gone unattended would have been a nuclear war that only a baby knows how to win. It would have been a blood bath.

So, I found myself feeding her with one hand while changing her diaper with the other. My left hand fed bits of carrot and lentils, and scooped up the leftovers from the corners of her mouth, while my right hand wiped digested peas and turkey from her creases.

Learning to do things with one arm is a skill that most parents master out of necessity. Being able to do this equally well with either hand is a skill that not everyone gets the hang of, but being that skilled with both hands at the same time makes me want to slap myself on the back in self-congratulations. And I would, if one hand wasn't full of lentils and carrots, and the other wasn't covered in shit.

On this particular day, I found that I'd even out done myself. I'd split myself in half and was able to handle two tasks simultaneously that were diametrically opposed. As sweat trickled across my brow and into my eyes, the panic suddenly turned to a tranquil meditative confidence, and I felt like a well-oiled machine. At one point it seemed like I was skillfully pushing fruit and veggies through one end of a food processor, and wiping up spills of baby poo with the other.

I somehow survived this once in a lifetime moment that convinced me I could do anything.

POOPiNG in the Bath

I was giving my daughter a bath the other night when she decided she just had to shit in the tub. I saw it happen in slow motion but I was powerless to do anything about it until it was already too late. I watched her body stiffen as she raised her self up to a half standing position. A soft grunt escaped from her mouth and she looked up at me and smiled. I leaned toward the edge of the water and heard my voice slowly drone "No!!!" to no avail. A few small golden nuggets floated to the top of the water and she giggled.

I just looked at her with my head slightly cocked to the right, and with a perplexed look etched on my face. I wondered out loud, "You just had to take a fucking dump now didn't you? Why didn't you wait until I had my arms full of groceries, elbows deep in dirty dishes or hands attached to power tools before you crapped!? You had that diaper on all day and you waited until now!?"

I pulled her out the water with one hand, and lifted the toilet seat with the other. I plopped her down on the edge of the toilet with just enough of her ass extended over open water, in case she had anything left to deposit in the bowl.

I held her in place and at the same time scooped out one turd after another with a Dora tea cup she keeps her Little People in, I dropped the oversized pellets of poo, behind her into the light green forest scented toilet water cocktail. The "bloop" sound of each shit stone splashing into the water made her laugh and kick her legs. I had to re-balance her before her warped sense of humor dropped her ass first into the toilet, among the brown stones of her last meal,

The whole time I felt like I existed outside my body, and I was calmly in control of a physical existence of me. I know that sounds like I might be writing this on acid, but what I guess I mean to say is I've rarely felt that in control of a situation. And it felt good. Because let's face it, most of those situations go terribly wrong, and it really feels amazing when it doesn't.

As I sit at the dinner table and draw this piece to a close, my daughter has again shit in the tub. My wife, knowing that I'm writing about this very subject has left the lily pads of poo floating in the bath for me to see. Was she trying to reignite the fire in this story for me, or was she hoping I'd clean it up for her?

My wife never saw it coming either. My daughter was floating on her belly pretending to swim, when bubbles burst behind her. They blew out her butt and floated to the top, and when they popped they smelled less like roses than skunk. When farts smell like shit, shit is soon to follow. But that kind of reasoning only happens after the fact. Looking back on it only serves to make you wonder that much harder how the hell you never saw it coming.

For a split second of comic relief, I thought about letting my daughter bathe in a stew of her own pee, snot and filth. And of course I never would have done that to my little peanut, but the thought of it made me laugh a tough day away.

It had already been a long day for me, and the wall of traffic that surged forward at five mph for the length of the entire highway had my nerves rubbed raw, so really what would've been worse, me falling asleep at the wheel for a second or two, on the way home from work, or her bathing in her own shit? I would have been road kill under the wheels of a big fucking truck. My daughter would have to endure a second bath to clean off the first one. So you have to excuse me if I laugh at the thought of her in shit speckled bubble bath. It's just that failing to pull her out of her bath before she soiled it, was the best part of my day.

Nursing in Public is Disgusting?

When did nursing your child in public become such a distasteful activity that causes some people to recoil and hiss? Why is it when you see a mom giving natural nourishment to her baby, it's more offensive than a toddler in her stroller sucking a big gulp through a straw? This can't really be what we've evolved into.

I realize there is a stigma in this country attached to seeing a bare breast in public, and of course, it doesn't help matters when the boob is pissing milk. But at some point in history this must have been a common thing to see, like someone clearing their throat, or raking leaves. I personally don't know what all the fuss is. I for one love to see bare breasts in public, and if I occasionally catch a glimpse of a boob leaking food into a baby's waiting mouth, I just write it off as a small price I have to pay to see bare breasts.

I personally don't know how you ladies get anything done all day. If I had beautiful mounds of flesh hanging off of my chest, I'd play with them from the time I woke up until the time I went to bed, and I'd never leave the house. And yet somehow you manage to work, and raise kids, and put up with the kind of guy that would stare at himself in the mirror for hours, if he had tits.

I myself was never nursed and so maybe my zest for breasts is just me making up for the lost opportunity as a baby, and trying to reconnect with my infancy, one boob at a time.

My son was a sucker until he was three. My daughter is nearly two and she still sucks. But if nursing for extended periods of time develops superior brain power and immune systems with retard strength, then my kids are the poster children for sucking teat, even if it means having to do it in public.

I give my wife a lot of credit because she doesn't care what anyone thinks. She knows how important nursing is for a child and doesn't care who sees it or knows it. Last Halloween my daughter and wife's costumes were Star Wars themed; my wife was Darth Vader and my daughter was Princess Leia. At one point, in the middle of a popular neighborhood for trick or treating, Darth Vader needed to nurse Princess Leia. The streets were so packed with parents and kids carrying sacks full of cookies and candy, the pavement was shut down to traffic. Darth Vader sat down on a curb beside a section of road that led up to the public library. She opened a hatch in her mobile life support system, and pulled out her boob. Princess Leia latched on and sucked for dear life.

Of course, the real problem in this country is that the question isn't should I nurse in public or not, it's should I nurse at all.

I used to work with this real straight-laced, clean cut guy who was about to have a baby, and he and his wife had decided not to nurse. He told me that he had done a lot of research and had found that using formula was actually better than using mother's milk. I had to put my hands in my pockets and squeeze my balls tight to keep myself from laughing in his face. I think they were both too terrified to be ridiculed and scorned by their straight-laced, clean cut family and friends, in the event that they were forced to nurse in public. I had to believe that his research was just a ruse to divert attention away from the truth, because nobody can be that stupid.

I understand there are moms who'd rather not breastfeed or in some cases just can't. Who am I to judge them? But please don't tell me that even the highest quality of organic formula can come close to providing a baby and child with the nutrients that mother's milk can.

I don't care what juvenile name you give to the milk in a mother's breast, be it tit tonic, boob broth, or jugs of juice, they're just never as stupid as the factory produced alternatives of Similac and Enfamil. I mean simulated lactation? Really? Pumping your kid with melted manmade mammary mud is perfectly fine, but nursing your kids in public, like every other mammal does, is disgusting.

Well, there you have it folks. Proof positive that breastfeeding in public is disgusting.

Even after kids my wife still has great legs

7

My wife just came down stairs with my daughter in her arms and both were covered in regurgitated noodles, chicken and peas. My daughter threw up all over the two of them in bed. I went upstairs and grabbed some new PJs for both and some warm wet wash cloths to wipe off the puke. After changing the bed I helped dress them both. As I was pulling a new pair of panties up my wife's long legs I paused in wonderment. Even covered in chunks of baby barf, my wife had managed to arouse me.

ALEX GOETCHIUS

Boys are Gross

#8

Boys are gross. I should know. I'm still one of them. I come from a long line of boys. My father was a boy; his father was a boy, and apparently my great, great, great, great-grandfather, who ruled his house with an iron fist, was a boy too. But I've never seen anyone who is more boy than my son.

Over the weekend my son and his friend were crammed in the back of my Mini Cooper, wrestling and giving each other Wet Willies. They wrestled for a while and then stopped to list all the things that boys like, that girls don't. There were bugs, gross stuff, bloody video games, shooting each other with Nerf guns, gross stuff, watching people do stupid things on YouTube, farts, poop jokes, picking your nose, gross stuff and especially giving Wet Willies. And with that, one of them stuck a finger, wet with spit dripping from its tip, into the ear of the other. Then they started to wrestle again. I gave a half-hearted "take it easy back there" and thought how amusing they were for listing "gross stuff" three times.

My son and his friend have a few variations on the standard Wet Willy. There's the Booger Willy in which your finger is injected into the deep recesses of your nose. Wet and sticky green things are mined from a nostril, and jammed into someone's ear.

If that isn't nasty enough, there's the Wax Willy. With the Wax Willy, instead of snot, it's the pasty discharge from your ear that clings to your finger. And then that's jammed inside someone else's ear. This is not only disgusting but ironic. You can actually clog someone's ear so they can't hear out of it, with the sludge from your own.

When there's not enough time for any of the more advanced variations, there's the Full Willy, where you just jam your tongue into someone's ear. The only problem with that is that boys are gross and never clean their ears, so there's always a chance of tasting someone else's earwax. Now let's not pretend we haven't all tasted our own earwax before. Surely there are some that find their own earwax a bit of a delicacy, much like some of us prefer our own farts to a flowery stick of incense. The rest of us however, have probably tasted it by accident. An itch on the inside of your ear, just above your brain, followed by a quick nibble on a finger nail and voila, an instant waxy appetizer.

Watching them wrestle in the back of my car and slamming wet fingers into each other ears reminded me of the horseplay we engaged in when I was my son's age. But when I was a kid we used to just pin a guy down by the shoulders with our knees, "hock a logy" and let the "ging-er" hang down above his face. Translation? We used to cough up some phlegm, let it drool out of our mouths and suck it back in at the last second, before it splattered on someone's face.

When I was a kid we didn't even know what Wet Willies were, so the first time my son gave me one I was totally caught off guard. Over the years, and the handful of Wet Willies my son has been brave enough to give me, I thought I had learned every variation there was to know. But apparently there was one variation I just never imagined.

That's when I looked in the rear view mirror and saw my son's friend stick his hand down the back of his pants. Fuck!!!! It was a Chocolate Willy!!!!

I slammed on the brakes and skidded the car onto the shoulder of the road. I pulled my son out of his seatbelt and into the front seat, before his friend could jam his nasty finger inside my son's ear. I told that brown fingered fucker that if he tried that again I was gonna drop him off at the curb, but I wouldn't be slowing down to do it.

I have thicker skin than my son's mom when it comes to the gross stuff that makes boys laugh. After all, other than a Chocolate Willy, there isn't a whole lot I haven't seen before. And because I'm still a boy at heart, in my mind and in my soul, I can appreciate the things that shouldn't, but do, tickle my son pink. But this ass to ear prank was more than I could take.

After we dropped Stink Finger off at his house, I told my son how much that kid freaked me out. My son is everything to me and I'd slay dragons for him, especially the ones with shit on their fingers. But apparently the dragon wears his pants too tight and his fingers never reached his "poo hole," as my son is want to call it. "Ah dad, he was just pretending," my son said. "I smelled his finger, it smelt fine." Good thing my son didn't let his friend stick his finger in his ear, he just smelled it instead.

I told you boys are gross.

Parenting is a tough job

Parenting is a tough job. It's an impossible task to do perfectly and one that is rarely done right. It's a job that those without kids can never understand and only underestimate. I know I did before I had kids. My friends without children try to relate, and think they can through their experiences with their nephews and nieces, dogs and cats, and impossible jobs of their own. But parents are battle tested and battle scarred creatures whose pain can only be felt by a fellow warrior parent. We weren't born parents so we have a decent perspective, being able to compare our lives with and without kids, even if some of us can barely remember what it was like B.C. Before Children.

I'm not trying to toot our own horns for taking on such an admirable task as raising children. I mean what person in their right mind knowing what we know now about raising kids, would ever want this thankless job. But in my estimation, the only thing harder than being a parent, is wanting to be one and not being able to.

The Girl Who Sings But Doesn't Speak

10

My daughter doesn't really speak so much as she sings. She sings in the tub and in the car and in her sleep. Even her deep and slow breathing while she dreams, is like a soft sparse melody. My daughter has discovered that the only way to be heard is to sing long and loud. Sometimes she'll let me sing along with her. Other times the message she's trying to convey is too important to allow me to screw it up for her. On those occasions she'll sing-song an animated battle cry, "No, no, no," until I stop. It's only her singing that can shut the loudmouths up.

You see, my daughter lives with three animated and passionate loudmouths who monopolize every conversation. My wife and son and I, at times can dominate, and even man handle the silence, until there's no room left for even one… more… word.

So my daughter sits quietly and drinks it all in.

She hears a lot of crazy chatter from the three of us shouting at each other. And she hears a lot of lunatic laughter at things that probably aren't funny to most other people. So she's slowly becoming the collaboration of three opinionated bigmouths who are completely out of their minds. And she's done this without much of an arsenal of words. She communicates almost exclusively in song and dance.

Don't get me wrong, my daughter speaks, and to be honest she has an endless wealth of things to say, and she almost never shuts up. But the thing is, she says it all in some kind of alien make-believe language that only she can understand. I know this because I hear her talking with her dolls and stuffed animals in our hollow house. Her make-believe words dance through the walls, and sound like cute and fuzzy animals chatting and giggling.

At some point, my daughter realized she'd never get a word in edge wise. Instead she sat quietly entertained and learned how to provide the musical score to this silly family's madness. But maybe it's worked out for the better. She's had the benefit of observing, then learning the art of conversation and debate, and the subtleties in waging a war of words. She's learned how to fight for a cause and defend a point, even if she hasn't had enough practice to say the things she feels. Instead the feeling behind her words pours out of her in song, dance, tears and laughter.

Recently my daughter has stumbled upon a single word that sums up everything she feels. It's a word that fills her deep despair and her jubilant fits of laughter. It's the one word that she says as clear as a bell, and a word that can only mean one thing, and yet means everything all at once. She sings it to the heavens and she'll stare you down and make you listen to her say it when she screams, whispers, sings and wonders "Wow."

ALEX GOETCHIUS

Liar, Liar Pants On Fire

11

My son just climbed up on the counter looking for hidden snacks. I asked him if he had finished his homework and he said yes, but I knew he was lying. Just as I finished uttering "Liar, liar pants on fire," he hopped down from the counter and sat on the stove. He accidentally lit the pilot light with his butt and burned a whole in the seat of his pants. That's the first time he's done that without having explosive noxious farts. Normally he burns holes through the seat of his pants from the inside out.

ALEX GOETCHIUS

This is who I am, Mom. Deal with it.

12

"This is who I am Mom. Deal with it. I like who I am, and I'll have funny stories to tell my kids." This is what my son said one afternoon after he had frustrated his mom beyond her breaking point. She finally yelled at him as she threw up her hands, "Why can't you be more like…" She stopped herself before she broke one of her cardinal rules.

As parents, we pray for the day our kids learn to like who they are, especially if who they are is a little different from everyone else. We wait for the day where they learn that we all feel this way; that we all sometimes feel like we don't fit in. And you hope they someday see that "everyone else" is just really billions of little missing pieces trying to fit in, just like them.

My son has gotten to a point where he finally understands that he's unique and a little different from everyone else. A lot of us are, and we wear it proudly, but that's a tall task for a kid who only wants to fit in.

You want your child to embrace his uniqueness and individuality because it'll be what makes him shine as an adult, and what makes him so special now. On the other hand there aren't many heartbreaks you suffer as a parent, more painful than watching your child struggle to make friends, because you let him wear his hair too long, or you let her play with trains. Or worse than that, because you let them be who they are. But **I don't think we're here to create or change who our kids are now, we're here to understand the person we've been given to protect, and help them become the best of all the possible "thems" they could be.**

My son doesn't fit inside a box. There is no sized box that can contain him and his gigantic swirling energy. No matter how thick the walls are that are meant to keep him in, he breaks them down with ease and runs free. He's smart enough not to stray too far from the box, as he runs around it in circles, and then bumps into it and falls down. He's also smart enough to have made a few friends on the inside, some of who wish they had the guts to escape as well.

What I've noticed recently is that my son has become more comfortable with his visits inside the box where his school resides, where his classmates' birthday parties are celebrated, and where his after school play dates happen. But no matter how comfortable he gets on his trips to the "inside", he'll always be just a tourist and a guest. But he seems okay with this and that makes me smile, and I know he's going to be alright.

"This is who I am Mom. Deal with it." We've definitely learned to deal with it, and now I'm glad he has too.

ALEX GOETCHIUS

No Matter How Rotten My Son is ...

13

No matter how rotten my son has been all day, and no matter how disappointed I am in myself for the way I dealt with him, his day always ends with a kiss from me on his head and an "I love you, you're the best kid ever," from my lips.

And no matter how bad of a day I've had, and how much I forget to give my son every last bit of me he deserves, my day always ends with my son squeezing my hand and telling me "I love you too, you're the best dad ever."

ALEX GOETCHIUS

You Raise My Kids. I Dare You!

14

Don't you just love it when people tell you how to raise your kids?! Especially total strangers and friends who don't have kids, or people who you're certain were never kids themselves. Go ahead and raise my kids if you think you can do a better job, I DARE YOU!!

I have friends who don't have kids yet they think they have some kind of insight into parenting because "I'm around kids a lot." Yeah well, that just makes you a potential sex offender. Or they say, "But I have nieces and nephews." Oh yeah? Come back when you have real kids. My favorites are my friends who try to equate having a "needy" dog to being a parent. They tell me how well behaved their dogs are and then try to offer up some K9 advice to apply to my kids. Shut Up! They're not human, they're dogs! "Well you're just saying that because you don't like dogs." I like dogs fine, what I don't like are dog owners who tell me how to raise my kids.

Even parents, or people who remember being one, have no idea what it's like to raise my kids, just like I have no idea what it's like to raise theirs. They have no idea what the last hour has been like raising my son, let alone that last 8 years. They can't fully comprehend what it's like to be me as a parent, or to have kids like mine. I don't expect them to. I can barely comprehend it myself, and I'm sitting in the middle of it and living every second of it. And yet, here they are anyway, telling me how I'm raising them wrong.

I've had parents tell him to "Shut him up" and tell me, "You better control your kid or I will." Geez people are so nasty to cute and innocent little boys who fart and curse and wipe their noses on their sleeve. They are cruel to the boys who spin out of control and laugh like a lunatic, and to those who talk too much but love a lot, and are generous to anyone who needs it. Christ, you'd think they never saw a human tornado before.

My wife and I put a lot of time and effort into raising our kids, and I'm sure we've made them a little nuts. But it's the kind of crazy we like, the kind of crazy we are, and we're alright with that. We're not going to beat ourselves up for letting our kids be a little nuts like us. We do the best we can with what we have to work with, even though we still make mistakes. We try to teach our kids right from wrong even while we're still learning that ourselves.

But lately it seems the more energy we exert, and the more we give a fuck, the less our kids hear us. It's gotten to the point now that our words fall over our son like a comfortable blanket of silence, and the only time he hears us is when we aren't saying anything at all.

Sometimes I'll stand right in front of him, look him in the eyes and repeat something to him over and over again. I like to count how many different ways I can ask the same question before I get a sign out of him that he's alive, a little recognition of my existence, and then even just a grunt for an answer.

Of course, with others, my son is so quick to answer he usually finishes their question for them. But with me I have to invent new voices and bizarre ways of speaking to get him to hear me enough to even blink.

So I think from now on, when someone tells me how to raise my kids, I'll just throw up my arms and bark back, " If you think you know a better way, show me, because I haven't got a fucking clue."

Whenever we can, we'll let other people discipline our kids. Total strangers are the best, because they pull no punches. Strangers tend to wait until they're at their wits end before they speak up, but when they do they can get ugly. So our kids will get to see the worst a person can be because of something they've done.

I'll say to them, "you know what, you're right! I am a shitty dad! Maybe you can show me how it's done."

Then I'll slip away and have a few cocktails while some stranger shows me what I'm doing wrong. They'll look back at me and tell me with their body gestures, "This is how it's done." And I'll nod in agreement as I lift another sip to my lips.

It will serve my son right for not listening to us. He should have respected how cool we are with him, and paid attention to what we were saying. Now he'll have to do it this stranger's way, and if he doesn't he might finally be forced to deal with a punishment he can't talk his way out of. "Who knows what kind of psychos my dad is letting raise us just to prove a point," he'll say to his friends.

So do whatever you got to do to help me discipline and raise my kids. Pull them by the lobe of their ear, between your index finger and thumb. Yell at them if you have to, and make them cry. Make them feel like shit for the horrible things they do to their parents that we somehow let them get away with. The only thing you can't do is beat them. That would bring DYFS to my house hassling me about how you're not able to control my kids, and how you're doing a shitty job raising them. And who the hell needs that.

celeBratinG 40 all Over aGain

15

My wife turned 40 a little over a year ago. You wouldn't know it by looking at her. She still gets proofed when we go out for cocktails. Of course it's a nice reflection on me because people always look at me and tell her how young her father looks.

Seven years earlier, my wife threw me a surprise party for my 40th with an Alice in Wonderland theme. Then we hopped on a plane and went to Greece.

When her 40th came I had just been laid off from work and we were just scraping by. I was selling blood and sperm and any other body fluid I could find a taker for just to pay the mortgage. So the thought of having a lavish celebration when we had no money to pay for it stressed me out completely. And the thought of NOT having the kind of extravagant celebration that my wife deserved filled me with sadness.

I promised her when we got back on our feet a few weeks later, I would have a belated party for her the likes no one has ever seen. But the weeks turned to months and the blood and sperm kept flowing while the pennies trickled in. If only I could have sold my angst.

Eventually my luck did turn and I landed a great job, and so on my wife's 41st birthday I threw her a beautiful 40th birthday party. All her friends showed up and the party raged on into the night fueled by wine, song and dance. There were many presents given and much love exchanged, but the nicest gift my wife received by her own admission, was the year I gave her back on her life. She spent the next 12 months getting to be 40 all over again.

Constipation

16

"This is hell! Satan will be coming any minute now!"

My son was struggling mightily to go to the bathroom, and I could hear him yelling this from two blocks away. I was on my bicycle coming back from the food store with a bag full of assorted laxatives and prune juice. The birds chirping a melodic cadence, and the leaves rustling in a cool breeze that came in off the ocean, were drowned out by my son's constipation.

It was a Monday morning and we were on our way out the door to school, when my son doubled over with cramps. I thought maybe it was just a bad case of gas as he triumphantly passed wind through a tuba mounted to a rusted muffler. But as parents, we're trained to walk around sniffing our babies' butts and the putrid air surrounds our farting children, in hopes of warding off some unfortunate accident. We get really good at recognizing when a harmless bout of gas is about to turn into something a whole lot more substantial, and soil a brand new pair of tighty-whities.

"Mercy!!" My son's pained plea for help shook the house as I rolled my cruiser up the driveway. He was trapped on the toilet with things moving around inside of him, but nothing moving out. With each passing push and each pass of gas he waited in agony for the mother lode.

"Shit my back hurts!" With his face beet red and belly bloated from mounds of indigestible cheese, my son looked like he was trying to push out a baby. I walked into the bathroom victorious like a knight on a majestic white steed, whose sword is raised to sky, With a bag in each hand I was armed with the necessary supplies to extract that festering blob of unborn mozzarella. I handed my wife the contents of each bag and told her it was time for us to induce labor.

It's hard to believe, the day before my son was wildly running around Chuck E. Cheese, chowing down pizza and bouncing off the arcade games like a pinball in a popcorn maker. Well I guess it's not that hard to believe it if you consider how thick and greasy, with mountains of melted cheese, the pizza was. You could've stomped on that pie with both feet and it would've stuck to your shoes like a huge gooey piece of bubble gum.

Toward the end of the night my son showed me all the arcade games he was able to hijack and cheat a few free games out of. I told him he had to stop doing that because it was stealing. He said he did it for me because he heard me complaining about how expensive the pizza was, and he didn't want to ask me for any more money for games. For all things my son is, funny and defiant, belligerent and intelligent, he is above all else gifted with a heart of solid gold. Oh yeah, and he's also a great bullshit artist.

Twelve hours later my son is trapped on the toilet and wedged in its seat, leaving a red ring around his ass that took days to fade. And there I am pouring prune juice and laxative cocktails down his throat, past gurgled protests and angry words that echoed through the neighborhood. "I wish Chuck E, Cheese never existed!!!"

ALEX GOETCHIUS

My son thinks soup is a finger food

17

My son thinks soup is a finger food. He eats everything with his hands as though he were raised by wolves that had access to a stove and oven. Even his two year old sister knows how to use a fork better than he does. She can perfectly spear each piece of her food with even an over-sized adult fork, and neatly chew it down into her belly, then wipe the corners of her mouth with a napkin. My son still uses his sleeve. If anyone sees boys shirts made from paper towels please let me know.

My wife still cuts my son's chicken for him and then places a fork in one of the pieces to give him a good head start. He'll eat all the pieces around it with his fingers, and leave the piece still attached to the fork on the plate.

Seeing this, my wife walks by, picks up the fork and shovels the last bit of chicken into his mouth. Good luck finding a woman who'll do that for you when you're older. I don't know if he has some kind of mental block when it comes to eating with the proper utensils or if he's just fucking with us.

I try not to use the "why can't you be like your sister" approach because I never want my kids to feel inferior in any way to each other. But just when I'm thinking to myself, why CAN'T my son have the same social graces as his sister, I see her eating her soup with her fingers.

Face Plant

 # 18

I took my son to the indoor skate park last weekend and he wound up face planted at the bottom of a wooden half pipe. For an instant it was the most horrifying thing I'd ever seen. I've watched a lot of video of really bad things on YouTube, but this was MY son smashing his nose on the ground at 20 mph, right in front of my eyes. For me that moment, that was harder to endure than any video I've watched in disgust or despair.

It's weird because I had this ominous feeling that something bad was going to happen when we first got there. It was a gray cloud that hung looming in my heart even though it was a warm and sunny day outside. It didn't ease my mind when my son tripped over his skateboard and crashed into the snack bar display window on his way to register for lessons. It felt like my son was way in over his head, as kids a couple of years older maneuvered around the skate park with a little more ease, and a little less recklessly.

The instructor of these "lessons" was well intentioned, but looked like he had just crawled out of bed after crawling into it not too many hours earlier. Each kid in the class was given a brief taste of instruction and then kicked out of the nest, and then expected to fly on their own without a hitch. My son tried a couple of kick flips onto a splintered platform, and then a couple of grinds across a one foot high rail. Each time he crashed it brought him a couple of inches closer to falling off the ramp altogether, and landing on the cold cement floor below.

Without much help from anyone else, and with balls as big as coconuts, my son figured out how to navigate through a moving maze of skaters . Down a ten foot drop he plunged, over a couple of ramps, and then back up the other side of a half pipe that slowed him to a stop. It was really a beautiful thing to see. I caught him doing it on video even though I felt like recording him might jinx him. I was partly afraid I might catch some horrific fall on video, but more than that I thought I might cause it.

And then he crashed. On the video you can see him land face first onto the floor, then jumbled madness as I raced from behind a mesh net wall that separated the dads from their sons. I bolted across a couple of ramps and slid down the last small one where my son laid on the ground. A little blood dripped from his left nostril, and a long welt formed across the right side of his nose. The instructor who got to him first, told me my son's nose was broken. The words sucked the life out of me, and I would have barfed if I hadn't been so busy keeping myself from passing out.

I picked him up and he wrapped his arms around my neck and his legs around my waist. He let out a cry filled with sorrow as much as agony, one that I'd never heard before. It was like he'd been wounded to his core, and even his soul was in pain. I sucked my own tears back into my eyes and swallowed them. Unfortunately, my hippie shoes with the soft leather soles wouldn't let me walk up the ramp I'd just so easily slid down. It was the only way out of this crazy labyrinth of mega ramps and quarter pipes, and with each step I took with my son in my arms, I slid back down to the bottom.

On the ride to the hospital my son held a bag of ice against his nose and rested his head against the backseat divider with his eyes closed. Soft whimpers came from his throat like wounded whispers. My daughter freed her arms, leaned out of her car seat and towards my son, and sang to him the whole ride there.

We waited in the emergency waiting room and watched some Murder TV on the Discovery channel. My son rolled himself over in an abandoned wheelchair, to an empty double seat. I sat down and he laid his head in my lap and we let the intrigue and horror of the program distract us from our own drama. There were real scenes of dismembered bodies wrapped in garbage bags, and sagging mattresses filled with pools of blood. And there were words that made us feel that this could happen to us at any time. That night while my son slept, it also distracted him from having pleasant dreams, and manufactured one of the worst nightmares he's ever had.

Finally, it was our turn to be seen by the doctors. But there was more waiting to be had in the examination rooms. A couple interns and a nurse came by, one by one, and asked us the exact same questions. I guess they wanted to make sure we had our story straight. My son and I whiled away the time by feasting on the basket of dumdum lollipops, and by looking at charts on the wall. I half-joked that the dumdums probably cost $5 a pop, and that even though the nurse said "help yourself. They're free," the tab from the hospital's billing department might suggest something different.

My son bounced from wall to wall, hyped up on a major sugar rush. He broke into song and dance over a chart that showed us how not to mistake different kinds of candy with over the counter drugs. The doctors came by and asked "is he always like this?" I guess they wanted to know if he had sustained some kid of head injury.

On the way over to the x-ray room my son admitted to me that the last time we were there, he might have faked his limp a little. He'd fallen off the swing set at the park after school and hurt his knee. He said "Mom freaked out so bad I didn't want her to feel stupid if it was just a bruise." I laughed and told him he'd have to pay me back the $1200 from his allowance for the next 27 years. The Radiology nurse found that amusing and chimed in "yeah, and in 10 years he'll have to start paying you back for cancer treatment from the x-rays."

What the fuck!? Are you kidding me!?!? "Do you really work here or did you sneak in off the streets and through the back door," I wanted to ask. I wanted to crush her for blurting out something so stupid and so insensitive. Instead, all I had were thoughts that rattled around my brain clothed in baffled anger. The pain those words caused me was the same pain I felt ten-fold, watching my son eat it face first on a lonely wooden ramp.

Just imagining your own child ever being that sick should be enough to make you drop to your knees and blow a kiss to the gods that they've only suffered a broken nose. But after already watching my son lay motionless on the ground, and then cry in my arms like a baby, all I could think about was how bad it might look if I wrung that nurse's neck with my bare hands.

ALEX GOETCHIUS

Breaking all the Bathroom Rules

19

Today my son broke all the bathroom rules when he "took a crap", ate snacks and played video games on my laptop in between wipes, all at the same time. He stripped himself naked and squatted with his feet on the toilet seat like a frog. He had a bowl of chocolate covered pretzels to his right on the edge of the bath tub. And my laptop sat in front of him perched on a small step stool my daughter stands on when she brushes her teeth. My son reached for pretzel and pissed on the keyboard of my computer.

I can't tell you how many different ways I wanted to yell at my son for all the different things he was doing wrong all at once. But instead I stood there watching through the wide open door in amazement, with my jaw on the floor. Some battles are worth waging, and some battles aren't worth a damn, and other battles still just turn to laughter. It's too bad no one ever tells us which ones are which.

Coach Kill-joy

20

"There's a whole lot of things you have to do in life, but this isn't one of them."

That's what I told my son, with my arm draped around his stooped shoulders, after he walked off the field during the first game of the season. Baseball is too slow of a game for his intense, pedal-to-the-metal energy. In between pitches he would turn cartwheels and spin around in circles in the outfield. As a result they plopped him out in the outfield away from the action rather than third or first base where all the action is. Instead of being able to knock down balls and make long throws across the diamond, to nip base runners by a step, my son became disinterested just standing like a tall weed in the outfield.

The thing is, my son really loves hitting and catching and throwing a baseball. He's good at it too, certainly as good as any other kid I've seen his age. But he's full of unbridled joy and has a hard time containing his overwhelming enthusiasm for everything, so he gets in trouble. Some parents, teachers and coaches are creative enough and patient enough to harness his joy, and use it to their and his advantage. But it's just easier for most people to dismiss his energy and label him with behavioral issues. Geez! Every kid I know has behavioral issues to some degree or another, that's part of being a kid. But my son's energy and presence are so big, everything he does is exaggerated, so he gets away with nothing.

Coach Killjoy used to stand next to him in the outfield to help him focus. "Stand Up!! Pay Attention!! Keep Your Eyes On The Batter!! Stop Spinning Around!!!" he'd bark at my son in an endless loop. "Pull Your Pants Up!! Put Your Shoes Back On!! STOP PRETENDING YOU"RE BLIND!!!! It didn't take long for some of his teammates to chime in.

With each command Coach Killjoy bellowed, my son lost a little bit of joy for the game. "I wish baseball was never invented," he would tell me. "I wish the guy who invented baseball would die!!"

"I'm pretty sure he's dead dude," I'd say.

"Good!" He'd shout back before I could get the last words out of my mouth.

The first game of the season was no more than five or six batters old when I looked over into the outfield and saw my son lying in a patch of clover gazing into the sky.

He was searching for four leaf clovers with his fingers while watching an animal parade of clouds pass by. "Get up and pay attention!" coach Killjoy burped.

Coach Killjoy positioned my son on the right field foul line just behind first base. The next batter squibbed a little dribbler down the first base line. The catcher picked up the ball as it knuckled around on the ground, and threw it over the first baseman's head. The errant throw plunked my son flush on the lower part of his stomach, just missing the family jewels. He doubled over for just a second, and he grimaced that pained smile he flashes when he's trying to hold back the tears. His sister who was just on the other side of the chain-link fence from her brother, wandered out onto the field, stood beside him and gripped his pant leg with her little fingers. My son leaned down and hugged her, and she grabbed his hand and pulled him from the field.

They walked over to the bleachers and my son buried his face into Mom's belly while his sister stumbled and fell, and found something pink and shiny in the grass to play with. Being seven is supposed to be fun even for the kid that no one understands. But for my son, baseball had been anything but fun.

ALEX GOETCHIUS

Parenting is so sexy

21

When my daughter was little and still just consuming mother's milk, my wife came down with a stomach virus which left her bed ridden for a day and half. Those 36 hours were harder for me than any job I've ever worked. Having to care for a newborn who up until then had only really known her mother's touch, was harder than the miles of white picket fence I painted in the hot summer sun as a handyman, and harder than unclogging toilets in the fast food joint I worked at as a teen.

I think I held up ok, and my daughter and I grew tighter and closer because of it. But the one thing I couldn't do was nurse. Still can't. For those 36 hours I held out as long as I could but every few hours I had to bring my daughter to my wife, who would nurse her. The sight of my wife with a hungry baby attached to her boob, while dry heaving into a bucket I'd placed on the floor, made me wonder if under all that baby and under all that sickness was still the sexy woman I'd married.

After my daughter finished nursing, I took her in my arms and wiped my wife's brow with a wet wash cloth, and fed her a couple of chips of ice. I looked at my wife as she closed her eyes and fell asleep, and there was that pale but beautiful woman I've always known, lying there and resting. I thought to myself, they should give medals of courage to mothers like my wife for having to deal with things no one should ever have to.

Riding the Potty train

22

While changing diapers has never been a problem for me, and the sight of peas, carrots and corn embedded in a log of baby poo has never caused me to hurl my own meal of peas, carrots and corn, I wouldn't mind getting past the occasionally shit I find on my fingers after changing a diaper. But let me just say one thing before we start to celebrate the fact that our toddlers are potty trained. The road to clean fingers is a long one, and the years that follow successful potty training are still filled with wiping up after someone else's dump.

My wife and son have been spending a lot of time trying to potty train my daughter. They're so enthusiastic and excited about it; they went to the library and took out every potty training DVD on the shelf. Titles like "The

Magic Bowl," "I'm a Potty Pirate," "Stop Shitting In Your Diaper!" "Your Crap Is In My Hair!" and "Where's My Fucking Valium!?" have been equally entertaining and educational.

After weeks of watching these DVDs, my wife and son decided to put them to practice. They popped on a DVD called "Bye Bye Poo," took off my daughter's diaper and set up her little pink princess potty, complete with a magic wand for a flusher that rang chimes when she flushed. It's hard to imagine that we'd want to take such a cute little toy like thing and fill it with toddler poo and pee, just so we can wash it out by hand. But I guess this is what we must do to distance ourselves from the early man that we evolved from, who crapped on the ground and wiped with leaves.

My son liked this video best because it was an old cartoon with crazy music and illustrations that were way over the top. They showed little cartoon baby private parts which made my son laugh like a hyena, and they sang gleefully about the hole where the poo comes out. Even though most of the video gave my son fits of hysteria, he absorbed all the useful information like a sponge.

During the entire video, my wife and son kept placing my daughter on the potty, encouraging her to pee or poo there. When a tinkle or plop sound was imagined by either one of them they quickly lifted my daughter and looked for a nugget or stream of pay dirt. Finding nothing they placed her back on Princess Potty and moved on to the next DVD.

One by one, they watched each video attentively, remarking on all the great techniques they were learning, and extracting each piece to the potty training puzzle. Back and forth they debated over which of the multitude of ways to potty train, they should try next. The debate became heated and my wife and son exchanged verbal threats and insults. Things started flying across the room as both of them attempted to plead their case. The debate escalated to near blows which freaked both of them out. They collapsed to the floor and huddled together in a sobbing heap, a blubbering mess.

In the meantime my daughter had quietly stood up and walked over to the corner of the room and shit on the floor. She started to dance and accidentally stepped in it, and then proceeded to leave little foot prints of poo all over the house as my wife and son chased after her. Months later I'm still finding myself on hands and knees cleaning up little hardened brown shit prints in the shape of my daughter's feet.

With my son it was a little easier. Armed with reams of paper towels, organic cleaner and gas masks, we let him make a few messes around the house until he started making them inside the toilet. But with each near miss my daughter has, my son cackles like a lunatic. His joy is so profound with every pee and poo that finds the floor he almost wills her accidents to happen before she can find the proper place to deposit her waste. I truly believe that left to his own devices, he'd be finger painting with the stuff in the name of art.

ALEX GOETCHIUS

Shit Mitt

23

My daughter was just standing on the couch and calls out to me "Daddy?" I look over and she's smiling sheepishly with her hand raised shoulder high. She must have stuck her hand down into her diaper and it was now covered in shit. She was wearing a thick mitt of it. I think to myself, it doesn't matter what I wash that hand with, dish soap, toothpaste, anti-bacterial medical paste, or gasoline, it's going to be impossible to get the stink out for a while.

Why is smooshing fingers in their own shit so fascinating to kids? Maybe there's something comforting in wearing a steaming pile of plop as mittens and socks. Maybe if they could, they'd cover themselves with it like a blanket. Or maybe they're digging for a toy they lost and think they might have swallowed. Toys are like money to kids, and if I lost a $20 bill and thought my kids had eaten it, I'd be rooting around in their poo too.

The BaBy sitter killer

24

One night not long ago we were greeted at the door by my son the Ronald McDonald Slayer. My wife and I don't get out much but when we do there's always drama waiting for us when we get home. This was certainly no exception.

Everything started out ok. We rode our bikes around town staring into store front windows and watching people in their cars. We rode along the beach through puddles left over from the last rain, before ending up at a new bar and restaurant for a snack and spirits.

The frantic phone calls from home came rapid fired from my son, not long after we started to feel like ourselves again. You know the way you felt before you had kids, before you were totally consumed by them until you couldn't remember what it was like to be anything other than a parent? That was the feeling that began to settle over us, when all hell broke loose at home.

The cocktails started the ball rolling but a couple of soft kisses to the neck, and the brush of fingertips against a bare thigh, carried us back in time. We mingled with our past, where the fingertips and kisses were allowed to stay up late and play.

But the phone calls from my son sounded the alarm that woke us from our dream. I swallowed back the last sips in both glasses while my wife fumbled for her phone, trying to answer the last of my son's calls of mayday. Then we paid the bill and peddled home.

When we got home my son told me that the baby sitter had her boyfriend come over with McDonalds and that she ignored his sister while she stuffed French fries in her mouth and spilled special sauce on the floor.

For better or worse my son believes McDonalds is evil and that Ronald McDonald is the devil. My son has seen Supersize Me half a dozen times and he's read all about the harm that Mickey D does to the planet. He probably overreacted a little bit when he started drawing pictures of him with a sword in one hand and Ronald's head in the other. But it's not really his fault; his crazy crunchy parents have brain washed him. Fucking hippies!!

My son used the ketchup packets that come with burger and fries to color the blood in his drawings, and scribbled "Take your cancer in a box somewhere else" and "Unhappy Meals Go Home!" all over his drawings. Then he pulled a dirty diaper out of the garbage and put it on a plate, and told the babysitter she'd be better off eating this.

Later my wife would sit with our son, and together they corrected the spelling mistakes he scribbled on his drawings.

After I listened to my son's side of the story, I told him I was proud of him. Not because I completely believed that his side of the story was the truth, the whole truth and nothing but the truth, but because he stood up for what he believed in, and he defended his sister and the house against someone he thought was a monster.

ALEX GOETCHIUS

I love you man on the telephone

25

I was holding my daughter as her tired eyes scanned over the images of the Doodle Bops dancing across the screen. She hugged my neck, yawned into my shoulder and quietly cried for mom. I gently kissed her face and whispered "I love you" in her ear.

My phone vibrated in my pocket. I answered and in a hush tone I said "Hello." I continued to gently kiss my daughter's head and whisper into her ear, while I carried on a conversation with a man on the other end of the phone. Back and forth I went. A whisper in my daughter's ear, out of one corner of my mouth, and a "Yes, I've tested web-based systems" out of the other corner.

But somehow I think I may have gotten confused when I said to my nearly sleeping baby that I had 17 years of experience as a QA Engineer.

I'm not sure but I may have told the hiring manager of a very prestigious telecom company that I loved him. If I did, I wonder if it will help me get the job. And if I do get the job, I hope I won't be working directly underneath him.

Kids Change Everything

26

Kids change everything, except maybe their underwear. For one thing, they make sleep more elusive than a four leaf clover, a needle in a haystack or Big Foot. Now that I have kids, I believe in sleep as much as I believe in the Loch Ness Monster. I defy anyone to find more pictures of me sleeping then there are of long, tall Nessie. Sleep is a myth that the weak of mind and the faint of heart do before they have children. Sleep after kids, is nothing more than a mirage, an imaginary oasis for those dying of thirst.

For me, having kids means meals are no longer drab nights out in fancy restaurants trying new and different combinations of exotic flavors. Instead my meals are now a fun and unpredictable adventure waiting to catch what food I can before it hits the floor. I can't afford to eat, and also put healthy food on my kids' plates. So during dinner I hover around the table, waiting for my kids to discard bits of their meal, like an opportune seagull sniffing out scraps. A good dinner for me could mean crust trimmed from a sandwich, left over peas and carrots which may or may not have been spit back into one of my kids bowls, the last piece of chicken or turkey fat, or a couple of bites of cold scrambled eggs. Sometimes before my wife can clear the table, and the kids have gone out to play, I'll pour the remains of dinner into a blender and suck down a chunky compost smoothie, with a straw the width of a garden hose.

For desert, soggy baby slobber biscuits are one of my favorite after dinner snacks. Now that I know how good they are, I wish I knew about them before I had kids.

Eating scraps has definitely kept my weight down which is good because I've pretty much given up caring about the way I look otherwise. I once gave a crap about what I wore or how coiffed and groomed I was. Now it's completely pointless to bother. Most of my money goes to diapers and private school tuition anyway, so even if I could afford new clothes for myself, I don't think I'd risk having them ruined with pee, poo, boogers and barf, before I've even taken off the tags. Sometimes I feel like my clothes are made up of my kids' expelled bodily fluids, instead of the material that's stitched on their labels.

When the kids have gone to bed at night, I sometimes like to watch a little bit of television to escape. I used to watch the edgiest of films before I had kids, but now I can no longer watch movies in which kids are killed, have terminal diseases, are abducted, get sniffles, paper cuts, or have a bad day. I can't watch a film if any of the previously described scenarios even happen during one of the coming attractions played before the film. In fact I can no longer watch anything but comedies for simpletons and kid shows; for fear that a child might stub his toe or over sleep. I just can't handle the drama. The angst that everyday life with kids brings, is all that I can stand without also having to absorb Hollywood's artificial tragedies.

Before I had kids, I used to think my parents were completely clueless when it came to raising us. I believed they had no idea what it was like to be a kid, and so they had no idea how to talk to us. But now that I have kids of my own, and have no more clue than my parents did, I've come to realize they didn't do a bad job at all. Believe me, my parents weren't perfect but when it comes to raising kids, there's never been a parent that's done it right yet. Seeing myself in my kid's eyes somehow makes it easier for me to believe that my parents probably were kids once too.

Except for the occasional pair of dirty underwear stained with skid marks, kids change everything. We do our best to assimilate our children into the lifestyle we had when we were childless. But invariably we adapt to their needs with much less resistance than they do to ours. And so dinner and the theater, cocktails at a rock club, breakfast in bed, and sex at noon give way to early blurry eyed mornings of oatmeal and Barney.

With all the things kids do to beat you down, I can honestly say that the one thing that's changed the most and for the better, is the amount of love I thought I had in me. What I thought was a shallow empty pool, instead is a bottomless well deep enough to bathe my kids in forever.

Roller Skating Casanova

27

We went to the roller skating rink tonight. The last time we were there my son taught himself how to skate on the very first lap around the rink. Granted he looked like a drunken chicken with wobbly knees as he flapped his wings to keep himself from falling down. In fact I could have sworn I saw feathers every time he slammed into the wall or crashed to the floor. Even with all the spastic flailing about, my son mostly remained on his feet, so technically he was skating. But to me he looked like he was learning to fly.

Tonight he taught himself how to inline skate. By the third trip around the rink he was dance skating backwards to hip-hop and metal, showing off to the ladies. Sweat dripped from the blond curls that framed his flushed red face. He mouthed the words to "Sexy and I Know It", as he shifted his hips from side to side and rolled past a smiling pack of teenage girls.

The pack of teens became a cackling gaggle of geese as my son began to fall, and he flapped his wings preparing to take flight His swiveling hips propelled him over the concrete wall that separates the skaters from the vending machines and the hot dog stand.

My mind immediately raced back to all the times, I've walked into walls, smashed my head against traffic signs and fell into puddles of mud while showing off to the ladies a little too much for a little too long.

Drinking Wine from a Sippy Cup

28

A couple of nights ago my wife and I were out to dinner with the kids and their grandparents, after my son's Christmas concert. We promised him ice cream and fries, instead of the traditional bouquet of roses. The combination gave him a wicked ache in the belly that would have felt no worse if he had swallowed petals and thorns.

My wife and I ordered two glasses of wine, but we spent most of our time too busy with our children running wild to drink them. They were burning off the last bits of their daily dose of excitement they have for being alive. Sometimes it seems almost heartless not to let them enjoy their lives while they still can. We lazily chased after them to make sure no one got hurt. We corralled them in just enough to give the appearance to the diners and the wait staff that we were in control of the situation. But really we were prepared to ruin the dining experience of the entire restaurant if it meant our kids would fall asleep on the ride home.

It had been one of those days for both my wife and I. Days like these are like seagulls full of scraps and garbage. They circle above waiting to take a crap on your head. So we were really looking forward to washing the day from our hair and clothes. We were going to do this by watching children scream, shout, and holler but not sing, their way through the holiday classics. And then we were going to have their grandparents baby sit them while we snuck in a date.

My wife battled the house all day with sucking and sweeping machines against a foe that is capable of messing itself up even when no one's home. Meanwhile I endured the two hour commute home from work that seems to drain my spirit at times, if not my wallet, one mile at a time. And so even a shared glass of wine at some theme restaurant in the mall has to be embraced when you have kids, because that might be the most romance you'll see for a while.

Eventually we wore out our welcome at the restaurant and so we packed up the kids and stuffed our leftovers into a doggy bag. We paid the bill and looked down at our drinks that were more than half full. Besides a small bowl of salty crunchy things, the wine had been the only thing my wife and I ordered, and there was no way we were leaving behind a glass and a half of paid-for liquid bliss.

To be able to afford to eat and drink now is almost a luxury. A couple of glasses of wine or a box of Enteman's walnut Danish ring have become the new vacation for the middle class. But I guess we should just be happy that no one's taxed the air yet. Unless of course you consider the coordinated pollution of the shrinking supply of oxygen, in order to sell us air filters and gas masks, to be a kind of tax.

We grabbed my daughter's Elmo sippy cup from one of our bags and poured her water into a potted plant on the floor beside the table. We mixed the cabernet and the pinot noir together in the sippy cup until Elmo was flushed blood red. I held the cup up to the light and saw the dark crimson blend of reds flowing through Elmo's body. I took a long drag from the rubber straw and giggled to myself how deliriously wrong this all was.

Afterwards, in the front seat of the car parked in a crowded lot, I secretly sucked one last sip of that tasty wine blend, from my baby's Elmo sippy cup. It was just enough wine to cut the edge that wild children can put you on, but I assure you, not enough to make me drive anything less than safely home.

In my life, I've taken wine out of bars that I'd been drinking in, sometimes just walking out with the glass in my hand in plain view. And I've certainly snuck wine into a bar when I was low on funds, and I'd refill my glass when no one was looking. But I'd never before stolen wine in the same cup my two year old darling daughter drinks her heavenly fruit juice from.

My Son's Tragic Comedy

29

Tonight my son spent the entire time doing his homework crying about it. At first it was just simple bitching and moaning. Quickly he worked his way up to sobbing. When he was halfway finished with his homework he was a blubbering mess. By the time he was finished he was in the midst of inconsolable wailing with streams of snot and tears running down his face and dripping onto his work.

All at once the crying stopped and my son looked up at me smiling and said "How's that for acting dad?" I spent the rest of the night acting like I didn't want to kill him. As great as his performance was, mine was better.

Parents are Great improvisers

30

Parents are the great improvisers. We have to be. At any given moment the landscape can change and we're left in unfamiliar, or worse, uncharted territory. We are the masters at preparing for the unexpected. And when the unexpected comes you better not be caught off guard, and you better be ready to think on the fly, adlib off the script and improvise on a brewing situation before your lack of creativity helps sabotage the day.

I remember taking my son to a really cool dance performance when I needed to call an audible at the line of scrimmage. The dancers were umbrella people floating in air, giant caterpillars larger than a bus and flowers from another planet that hiccuped and burped whenever they bloomed.

But my son didn't give a rat's ass about it, he was bored to tears and let everyone on our side of the theater know about it. He was hot and hungry and completely over stimulated, and he protested by lying in his seat upside down with his legs in the air. The entire theater was treated to my son's running dialogue that echoed through the quiet moments of the performance.

I peeled him from his seat, I filled his belly with food in the lobby, and cooled off his skin and his overheated brain by walking around outside the theater. After a while we went up into the half empty mezzanine and he laid on his stomach in the aisle in just his pants, and stared at the stage hypnotized in amazement.

Parents are the great improvisers because on any given day you can wake up, and overnight all of your son's shoes stopped fitting. Overnight your daughter's taste buds have flipped 180 degrees and now she won't eat all her favorite food you just stocked up on. And of course you don't find out any of this until you're feeding or dressing your kids as you try and rush out the door.

The play date you set up with your son's best friend is now with his mortal enemy. The blue hair, blond eye dolly that your daughter begged you for a week ago, and the only doll you packed on your trip, is now no longer worthy of being played with. And that's probably only because it doesn't have brown hair and brown eyes.

I once took my son into New York to audition for a play and then go to a toy store. Toward the end of our day my son told me he felt like he was "gonna crap in his pants." I picked him up and put him on my shoulders and galloped past the horses just south of Central Park, looking for a bathroom to use. With each bounce he farted on the back of my neck and I prayed that's all it was.

Before he erupted down the back of my shirt, I found a Starbucks across a busy street. I darted in and out of traffic, bolted through the front door and got him on the bowl just as the flood gates opened. That's when I noticed there wasn't a stitch of paper to be found. No toilet paper, no tissues, no paper towels.

My son's first explosion ricocheted off the bottom of the bowl and splattered all over his ass. The second wave shot out between his legs and all over my sleeves. People started banging on the door as a long line formed. My head was so hot you could have cooked on it, and little pools of sweat began to form on my brow. Sweat dripped into my eyes and without any paper products around, other than a small piece stuck to the bottom of my shoe, I wiped the burning sweat from my face with my shit stained sleeve.

When my son's final blast was over, I did what any creative, forward thinking, innovative parent would have done. I cleaned him up with his socks and underwear and tossed them in the garbage.

Parents are the great improvisers, innovators and inventors. It's not to say you can't be any of these if you're not a parent. I'm just saying you can't be a decent parent without being any of these.

Celebrity Stalker

#31

This weekend I dropped my son off at his friend's house for a rousing match of celebrity stalker. My son's friend is a bit of a jock and my son loves guns and gadgets, so they sometimes don't see eye to eye when they get together to play. My son complains loudly to his friend, "all you ever talk about is basketball this and football that!" Of course, I then hear my son's friend yell back at him, "All you ever talk about is guns!"

This weekend was no different when we showed up at his friend's front door. He had just finished watching (ironically) celebrity skeet shooting with some famous football player, and wanted to go outside and throw the football around. My son rushed through the open door and made a b-line toward the Nerf gun bin in the playroom. Immediately the tension mounted, and I could see one of their monumental tear-flowing, fists swinging "disagreements" brewing.

My son and his friend make good sparring partners and have for their entire lives. They've known each other since they were born three months apart. Even then you could see them laid out on a baby blanket mugging up to the camera and elbowing each other for position.

Before the drama built any significant steam, their squabble grinded to a halt, when they agreed upon a compromise. The art of compromise is a major lesson we struggle to teach our kids. It's a useful tool to help get you through the day since most of our lives consist of compromise. The roads we travel are paved with all the concessions we've ever made. We want to teach our kids how to work together while still maintaining their individuality. Yet another impossible task the gods have handed down to parents.

As I drove off, my son's friend was signing autographs for imaginary fans, and my son was lying in wait, with a Nerf gun cocked, quietly hiding in the bushes.

Gourmet Scraps

32

I eat scraps for most of my meals, because it's either that or I walk around the neighborhood holding a sign that says "Will Work For Food." Over the last year my grocery bill has exploded, so instead of eating meals I follow my kids around the house with a plate in one hand, a fork and knife in the other, and a cloth napkin tied around my neck.

I've eaten food from the floor that one of my kids has dropped and forgotten about. Sometimes these tasty morsels are still pretty soggy. The more the scraps dry before I find them, the more they taste like the cookies or pizza they once were, and less like the slobber inside the mouth of one my kids.

I've gnawed on bricks of macaroni and cheese and wilted carrots and celery sticks. I've forced down half chewed broccoli crusted chicken that was too big for them to swallow, so they spit it back out onto their plate.

I've snacked on crackers and pretzels wedged between the cushions of the couch, and gulped backwash cocktails from the bottom of juice boxes. I've eaten food that has long since turned cold, after it's been cried on, and sneezed and coughed at. And I've probably eaten food that's been handled by dirty hands after my kids have wiped their ass or picked their nose.

When I walk in the door from work each night, I grab my kids and hug and kiss them like it's been weeks since I've seen them last. I pluck crumbs from their clothes and steal bites of food they might be holding, when they're not looking.

I suppose I could eat real meals but then I'd have to keep the house cold this winter, or sell my car and bike the 50 miles to work and back each day. Scraps are free because you're just going to throw them out anyway. And they're plentiful because kids are always going to make them. Long lost leftovers with a side of clumps of dusty crumbs, is a meal I can afford, from food I can't afford to throw away.

For the most part I love being a father and the bread winner in my family. It's what a man is supposed to do, so I do my best to do the right thing. But every once in a while, the daily sacrifices we make to be decent parents, are more than I can take. It makes me want to scream into a stack of pillows, or run outside in the quiet of the night and curse the heavens. Or worse, run straight for the nearest pub and blow my weekly allowance on a mug of beer and French fries.

Today my son stabbed a tangerine with a pencil after I "tortured" him for a while with algebra. When he pulled the pencil out of the tangerine's fruit, the point was missing from its tip. I tore out chunks of the tangerines flesh with my fingers, looking for the tip of that pencil. I found nothing but seeds and pulp. The juice ran down my arms as I held each chunk up to the kitchen light for close examination.

I dropped each piece of fruit onto a pile of tangerine guts, at the bottom of a bowl. I poured in the creamy nut pulp left in the last few sips of some almond milk, and sprinkled over it crushed up bits of hardened buttered waffles. I tied a napkin around my neck, whipped out my fork and knife, and ate like a king. And I may have even done all that with dirty hands after scratching my ass or picking my nose.

ALEX GOETCHIUS

Broken shoe

33

I brought a pair of shoes to the local cobbler over the weekend and he just laughed at me. He ran his fingers over the worn down sole and then the vanishing heel and laughed again, this time louder.

He said in a thick Hungarian accent "a man who brings in a pair of shoes like this to be fixed must walk around with holes in his underwear." He held the shoe up to his ear like a conch shell and closed his eyes. I asked him, "Why are you pressing my shoe to your face?"

He let out a long slow hush from his lips, pulled the shoe from his face and held it to my ear, and said "Listen, do you hear that?" I shook my head no, and he said "It's telling you to buy a new pair of shoes, and probably some new underwear as well." I could still hear him laughing as I closed the shop door and walked down the street to the other side of town.

Teachers are Only human

34

Teachers are only human, except for the really bad ones who are robots and puppets. Unfortunately, we have an educational system that is full of robots and puppets that become cogs in the machine. They are in constant recruit of fresh meat. Once they get the taste of a young teacher that still gives a shit, it's hard not to want to make them their dinner.

Teachers that actually don't become some puppet's meal or a robot's appetizer, take on the huge responsibility of helping to shape the future. It's a responsibility that isn't proportionately compensated for, and one that doesn't garner the proper amount of respect. Despite this great responsibility, this special breed of human is no different than you or I. Like us, they're marred with flaws and foibles, and given to all the vices man can offer.

At any given moment a teacher can be out late sipping too many cocktails and cavorting with the wrong crowd, gambling their paychecks away, or laying spread legged bathed in waves of ecstasy. Teachers fart and pick their noses just like anyone else. They're no different than us except they have taken upon themselves, for little or no recognition, the act of helping the rest of us be better people.

The responsibility placed upon teachers cannot be understated. They impart wisdom on the next generation who will provide for us when we're too old to drink, gamble and fuck.

The problem is that most teachers are not human, but robots and puppets. It wouldn't surprise me if most of those who run on batteries or pull strings were once human themselves. But the relentless battles against a failing educational system, wears them down until it's just easier to give in and turn the cruise control on full blast.

It probably doesn't mean they care any less, it's just that they're too tired and beaten down to do anything about it. Who can blame them? Day in and day out they swim upstream against the roaring rapids of administrative bureaucracy and parental interference. Who can blame them for giving up and letting the raging river swallow them up?

Being human, hung over with bills to pay and in failing relationships, is what makes the accomplishments of a good teacher so amazing. They put their own problems on hold and conquer those rapids every day. They never give in, and they'll die trying to save just one child from falling prey to complacency.

Maybe if we looked at teachers as being more human we wouldn't put so much pressure on them in an already thankless job. We'd take responsibility for our kids' education, and give these teachers something better to work with. But until then, we pray our kids find at least one teacher who cuts through all the bullshit life throws at them, and in the end leaves behind a lasting legacy of making a difference. If even just a little.

ALEX GOETCHIUS

How cool is my wife?

35

How cool is my wife?! She bought me a writing workshop in New York City last night. The instructor was Cullen Thomas and the workshop blew me away. The weather was a balmy 60 degrees on a January afternoon and felt more like one of those days that suggest the cold and bitter winter is over. I took a walk at lunch through the union square farmers market and then down Broadway to Forbidden Planet to stare at all the colors.

My wife, on the other hand, spent the entire day single-handedly fending off and surviving the nearly lethal drama conjured up like demons from our children. A full day with this army of two small children clearly had her out numbered. But somehow against all odds she outlasted the will of our son and daughter. For this she will be aptly rewarded with a Sunday morning sleep-in, some decadent chocolate from the city, and a passionate and sweaty romp in the hay the next time the kids are in school.

Now, while my wife sleeps exhausted, I sip from this glass of wine I stopped for to celebrate my day, and put an exclamation point on the end of it. Before I leave, I'll drop to my hands and knees on the dirty floor of this local pub. And with you here as witness I'll thank my lucky stars, the heavens and the gods, to have my wife to travel through life with.

Compassion for the misfit kids

36

Last week a kid in school puked on my son's brand new winter jacket. The jacket was a present from Santa and the puke was courtesy of Burger King. This is the third time the kid has thrown up in school this semester but the first time he's gotten it on someone else's stuff beside his own.

My son actually got in trouble for it. He was told "at least five times," of which he probably heard none, to grab his jacket from under the table where the boy stood. My son tunes out what he doesn't want to hear. Telling him to do something he doesn't want to do, or something he didn't think of himself, is like whispering into the wind.

The message is blown into billions of tiny pieces and in a million different directions. In the end, the message is either scrambled or it's never delivered.

My son is always getting in trouble for shit he doesn't do. But that's because he also gets in trouble for most of the mischief he causes. He's kinda the "bad-ass" of the school, if there is such a thing in a small farm schoolhouse with goats and llamas and chickens that run free. Because of this he doesn't get very much of a benefit of the doubt. Some of the kids like to use that against him and blame him for some of their own childish evil ways. But I know in his heart my son means well. He's a really sweet kid and truth be told, I can only dream of being as caring and generous a person as he is. That's how I judge his character and not by how delighted he gets when causing mischief, or how delighted others get when he takes the fall.

The coat of the boy who puked in school took the brunt of the bile, and shielded my son from the lion's share of the vomit. The school washed both together in a dirty jacket stew. Chunks of half-digested chicken French fries spilled out of both coats' pockets, and swirled around in its wash cycle, with a suds and soda chaser. Even though the brand new Christmas winter jacket was only slightly splattered, and even though it had been washed once at school and once at home, my son said he'd never wear it again.

But that's where I draw the line. Having to buy him a new jacket because he was too stupid, or too lazy or too spaced out to move his coat out of the line of fire, is the point where I stop becoming "the best dad ever." I tell my son, "I'm pretty cool about a lot of things you get in trouble for, but when you start costing me money, when you force me to get creative by spending money we don't have on things that we don't need, then that pisses me off."

Some people might say that I'm too lenient with my son, maybe even too forgiving. But as I try to teach my son the way of the world, I'm learning too. Every day there's something new I learn about him. And that's made me realize he's already who he is, long before I gave my two cents on the matter. I don't think we're here to create or change who our kids are now, we're here to understand the person we've been given to protect, and help them become the best of all the different "thems" they could be.

The boy that hurled all over my son's jacket comes to school each day with the best food substitutes that Dairy Queen, 7-11, Burger King and Dunkin Donuts have to offer. His lunches are made from chewy plastic food textures dunked in vats of manufactured flavor. His oh so anticipated desserts are doughy rubber chewy chunks, submerged in creamy baths of melted sugar. The poor kid doesn't stand a chance.

But it's not his fault. Somewhere along the line this just became the norm and it's all he knew. My son told me the boy had chicken French fries for lunch that day. He animated the slogan in a loud booming voice, with wild eyes and flailing arms.

"Just grip, dip and go! Wasn't that easy?! Take THAT, yoga class!!" Now I know some of you don't want to hear this next shit, but here it goes anyway. We've become a people who need to take a shot at health, just to sell food that will make you feel cool at the risk of feeling well. Soon we'll be sold things that make Angioplasty, Mastectomy and Chemo Therapy hip. And that will be just the tip of the iceberg.

My son's school is an interesting collection of public school "misfits." They are the cream of the crop of those who would never survive in public school but thrive in private. With that, you have a collection of kids who don't fit the mold in their very own different and special way. I think it's good for kids to be exposed to lots of people that are different from them, so they learn tolerance and understanding of just how diverse people can be. It helps them embrace their empathy for and devotion to the underdog. And it lets them know that It's okay to be different. In one way or another we all are.

My wife and I have preached this to the high heavens and our son gets it. Our constant ramblings on the topic have somehow cut through the wind, in voices much louder than whispers. It's important to have compassion for those watching life's party go on without them from the outside. Because no matter who you are, you'll find yourself at some point on the outside looking in.

Today my son taught the kid who puked on his jacket how to roller skate, at a birthday party of a classmate. It didn't matter that my son had just taught himself not more than 15 minutes earlier how to circle around the track without breaking his ass. My son wanted to share something new and exciting with the boy. Even though the boy had left an indelible impression on my son with respect to his nice new jacket that he'd never wear again, my son had forgotten all about it. He's big on forgiveness, and is all but a stranger to holding a grudge. He understands as well as anyone else that everyone is different. And he's found out first hand, it doesn't take much to be the one on the outside of life's festivities, peering in.

ALEX GOETCHIUS

A mental note written with invisible ink

37

Tonight my son asked me to make him toast for a snack before bed. I tossed a couple of pieces of bread in the toaster and promptly forgot about them. It's easy for me to let things slip my mind, because after years of over indulgence I don't have the same short term memory that I used to. My son likes to try and take advantage of that by insisting he's already done his homework or brushed his teeth.

I should have known by the smoke billowing out from the kitchen, the high pitched smoke alarm and the water sprinklers that flooded the floor that the toast had long ago turned to charcoal. The firemen who kicked in my front door and sprayed down my kitchen to extinguish the fire should have been a dead giveaway that my son's toast was probably ready and then some.

As time marches on I find myself writing notes on everything I own in order to remember things I shouldn't forget. I'm sure at some point I'll develop ink poisoning from all the messages I've written on my hand. I've even noticed the cat's look of concern when he darts off under the couch as I approach him with some hair clippers and a sharpie.

It's funny because I catch myself thinking "I should make a mental of that," but unfortunately my mental notes are written in disappearing ink.

My son thinks my face is a Dartboard

38

It seems my son shoots me in the head at least once a day. Sometimes he nails me in the middle of the forehead with a dart gun, or in the eye with a Nerf rocket launcher, or deep in my ear well with a stream of water from a super soaker. I think my eyes are his favorite target though. They must look like little bulls eyes to him. Once he locks his radar in there's no turning back. He has no kill switch to disengage the automatic firing system, and so at that point it's really out of his control.

I never see it coming until it's too late to do anything about it. But then time slows down and that's all I see, a suction cupped dart or a jagged stream of water explode against my eye. And all at once time races back to real time and the pain lingers for a few seconds disguised as numb shock.

I crumple to the ground and grab for my eye. My first instinct is to feel around the floor for it and hope that the insane pain I feel is from a punctured eyeball rather than one squashed under foot. Being hit in the eye is the closest thing I can think of to being kicked in the balls. They are such vulnerable parts of the body with almost no protection. The thought of popping either an eyeball or a testicle causes me to wince more than from the actual blow of either.

Tears fill up my eyes and overflow onto my face. It's the only way an eye knows how to save itself from dying. I curl up in the fetal position and hold my knees in tight against my chest, not just to absorb the blow by transferring pain to the rest of my body, but to hold myself down and keep me from killing my son.

I restrain myself enough for him to live to see another day, but the gun suffers a terrible beating. The last time he shot me in the face was with a remote control robot that shot round disks from its chest. He snuck up behind me and fired it point blank into my eye. I grabbed the little fucker, not my son but the robot, and threw him into the dumpster we have in our driveway for construction material, shit we're never gonna use again and fucking toys that shoot me in the eye!!!

Of course I couldn't just leave the robot alone, to die a nice quiet death with the rest of the trash, I had to first slam it against the driveway a few times and smash it into parts, to show it who was boss. But after its foot broke loose and kicked me in the eye, I'm pretty sure it knew it was more boss than I could ever be.

Time and time again I utter these preposterous words, "I will buy you this gun ONLY if you promise not to aim it at anyone's head." I guess it's my unwavering love for him that keeps on giving him another chance. His promises are so sincere, and I just want to so badly to believe him when he says, "I promise dad. I love you. You're the best dad ever." I know he means ever word he says. I also know how truly sorry he is when he breaks his promise again, and temporarily blinds me or nearly pokes out my eye.

ALEX GOETCHIUS

A letter to the kid who fell off his bike

39

I went to the mailbox this morning and found a letter in the mailbox that my son had addressed "To the kid who fell of his bike." I opened it up and read it, and here's what it said. "Some bad person posted a video of you falling off your bike on YouTube. I feel bad because the name of the video was called Fat People Falling. You are a brave kid." Along with the letter was my son's favorite Pokemon trading card.

I showed it to my son and he told me about the video. He said the person kept on recording even while the little boy cried for his mommy. My son choked up on the "Mommy" part and started to cry and didn't stop until I hugged him long and hard. Say what you want about my kid, there's no denying how big his heart is.

Hey Dad, Let's Wrestle

40

"Hey Dad, let's wrestle!" When I hear those words no matter how tired I am, or what foul mood I might be in, I just can't resist grappling with my son for a while. It usually burns off any excess energy he has before bed, and most of our battles end with both of us on our backs laughing. I usually start on all fours or up just on my knees as he bounces up and down on the couch, preparing to pounce. All at once he flings himself from the springy cushions and hits me hard. Sometimes he knocks me over, especially when I'm not quite ready and haven't braced myself for impact. My son leaps at me with so much joy that spills from his wide eyes and gaping mouth, how can I deny him this much pleasure even if it means a couple of bruises and the occasional kick to the groin.

At times the battles can get pretty ugly. We spit, punch, kick, pull hair, pinch, bite, flick the back of the ear, shove a finger in the nose, tickle, fart on and burp at. There's also the fake outs to get out of a hold. Sometimes my son will pretend to be hurt or pretend to have to go to the bathroom to get out of an imminent pin. Even though at that moment I am his opponent and arch enemy, I'm first and foremost his protector, so naturally I let him out of my death grip. He returns the favor by yelling "Sucker!!" and pounces back on top of me.

Actually there's not a whole lot of what we do that resembles wrestling. There is the occasional pin that happens almost incidental to everything else. The rules of what constitutes a pin change all the time depending on who's doing the pinning. If I'm on top pushing my son's shoulders to the ground, I have to hold him flat , say "one two three, Dad is the winner!", and slap my hand on the ground before he wiggles free. If there's any variation in that sequence then it's not a pin. And believe me there's always a variation, some real and some the product of my son's wild imagination. He can always find the one micro imperfection in the sequence, even if he has to make them up, to avoid the dreaded pin. I usually let it slide as long as he's put up a good fight.

There are so many other lessons to be learned by the little guy, I just don't have the heart to kill his buzz and get all preachy on him about playing fair. Life isn't fair anyway so why delude him. Somewhere down the road when he's older and life has his shoulders pressed to the ground, he won't just take it. He'll fight back with a flick to its ear or a punch to its groin. Maybe he'll let his imagination take control and fake his way out of it. Or maybe he'll just tickle it and learn every now and then to give life a little laugh. After all, your opponent is never quite as dangerous when they're laughing.

ALEX GOETCHIUS

contact lens

41

I just found a dried up contact lens on the stairs leading to the second floor of our house. I was amazed it wasn't crushed. I wanted to show my son, who was standing right there, because he's always very curious about mysterious things like contact lenses.

Of course when I wasn't looking he tried to put it in his eye. It got lodged behind his bottom lid under his eyeball. The pain was unbearable and he cried like a baby, which of course wet the lens, centered it on the eye and made it easy to take out. Suffice it to say contact lenses are no longer a mystery. Good thing I didn't hand him a hand grenade. He would have blown his head off trying to put it in his eye.

ALEX GOETCHIUS

Evil Dads Don't Let Their Kids Watch TV

42

I'm a mean son of a bitch of a dad because we don't have TV, and I should be drawn and quartered for it. The cruel and inhumane punishment has been part of my daily ritual of abuse since before my kids were born. I practiced these sessions of torture on myself to perfection, so I could inflict the maximum amount of TV-less damage on my children. I AM A MONSTER!!!!

Someone actually just tried to tell me this, with wild eyes and spit coming out of the corners of his mouth. He shouted at me saying I should be ashamed of myself because my kids would be ostracized and pointed at as freaks if they weren't current with the trials and tribulations of the fake lives of sitcom people, or hip to the lasted flavor of cool clothes and gadgets.

This guy continued to berate me for not letting my kid watch SpongeBob, "Oh wait, you probably don't know what SpongeBob is!" Of course I know what SpongeBob is. It's impossible to not know what anything on TV is. Television is like a sweet stink that finds its way under your nose, no matter how tightly you seal the windows and doors, and no matter how small the cracks in the walls and floor boards are. Once you get a good whiff of the candy scented stench you're hooked, and the smell takes a long time to wash out of your clothes and from inside your nose. After a while the stink becomes a familiar friend and you don't even bother trying to wash it off.

I attempted to calm this mad man down before his head exploded by telling him that we had a TV, we just don't watch TV. We watch DVDs that nurture the soul rather than pollute it. I should have known that this would only fuel his fire, and I guess part of me hoped it would. But rather than continuing his verbal assault on me, he simply said "Oh, you're one of those," and walked away.

Look, my wife and I got rid of television years ago because we happily let it suck us in for hours on end, and we'd do nothing else day after day. But our lives became richer once we cut the cable, because we were doing instead of watching. We traveled more, she opened a yoga studio, we started a band, and I wrote books. Hey, but don't get me wrong, I still love TV as much as the next guy. Its blissful addiction is like a drug or like sex, but you don't see those in control of me either.

The thing is, when we don't watch TV on purpose, it becomes a treat when we stumble upon it. I discovered Arrested Development on a business trip and Curb Your Enthusiasm on vacation. Part of a nice holiday for me is falling asleep watching TV. But I don't plan my day around it. I just can't afford to crave all the things that TV tells me I need to have.

So yeah maybe I am a little mean for denying my son SpongeBob on demand, but if this guy thinks I'm mean now, wait until I tell him we don't eat McDonalds either. Just stand back when I do, so you don't get little bits of brain on you when his head explodes.

ALEX GOETCHIUS

Biting Nails

43

Sometimes I find myself angry and frustrated or just plain sad and I take it out on someone I care about who doesn't deserve it. Usually they never see it coming. It's bad enough to take it out on a perfect stranger, but it sucks a whole lot more when its someone you love. Sometimes it's just hard to own your mistakes.

All my life I bit my fingernails. It was a nasty habit for sure that I never bothered to try and break. It seemed like a natural response to a sudden jolt of emotions to my system. After my son was born I stopped cold turkey the first time I saw him bite down on one of his own nails.

My emotions have always been trapped deep inside. They come out in passionate bursts of lightning and thunder every now and then, but really just stew inside me. Now I see those same bursts explode from my son. So, I've been doing whatever I can to own up to my mistakes and stop my jolts of emotion from storming out of control, so my son learns never to bite his own nails.

Candy Coated Karma

#44

There's a really cool shop in town called Atomic, which is home to vintage toys and clothes, pop art and collectible vinyl. My son and I have been going there since the very first day they opened. I have a pretty vast pop art and vintage toy collection, and the eye candy on Atomic's walls and on his shelves is enough to give your eyeballs cavities.

Atomic is run by Eric, a jolly guy in his mid-40's who has somehow escaped the grind of a 9 to 5 job that most of us "suckers" are trapped in. Occasionally the stress of having to make a living selling second hand stuff, which people have already given up on once before, gets to Eric. That's when my son and I walk into his shop and find him a little less than jolly. You can see Eric try his best to be cordial, but once my son goes into his routine of pulling anything new off the racks, and climbing the shelves to grab things high up on the wall he hasn't seen before, Eric starts to crack. And once he cracks he'll do just about anything to get us out of his store.

Once when my son was having one of his "human tornado" moments, Eric really began to unravel and suggested loud enough so my son could hear, that I take him across the street to the candy store. In fact I think his exact words were "Why don't you ask your dad to buy you some candy?" That was fucking brilliant on his part. A tactic he had yet to deploy and one I never saw coming.

The candy store in town had the worst of the artificially preserved man made fragrances and flavors money could buy. My son's favorites were the candy-coated cancer drops, and the cherry flavored embalming fluid that comes in a mouth spray. I do my best to steer my son away from the candy store whenever possible, because even the handmade chocolates taste stale and kind of moldy.

Over the years the candy store has changed hands from one chocolatier to another, and even as the handmade chocolates became more exotic, with chai tea chocolate Buddhas, and white chocolate truffles infused with spices, herbs, roots and flowers, they still tasted stale. Now the candy shop is a toy train store, and my guess is the trains there taste stale too.

I would have been upset with Eric's suggestion to my son that I take him candy shopping, if I hadn't been so impressed with how devious that suggestion was. But in the end, the universe evens things out.

Now when my son and I go into town and we wear out our welcome at the skateboard shop or in the dollar store, the clerk will suggest to my son "Why don't you ask your dad to take you to Atomic."

ALEX GOETCHIUS

the Playroom

45

How is it by the time that I've straightened up all the toys on one end of a not very large playroom, my kids have already destroyed the part of this ever shrinking room that I started on? A room this small, or any room for that matter, becomes hard on the eyes when the toys are all scattered across the floor, hanging off shelves and bulging from drawers that just won't close.

But more than that, a playroom can become a mine field of hidden toys buried beneath a pile of clothes, or wedged between the cushions of a couch with only the sharp pointy side of the toy poking through, as if someone perfectly purposely placed it there. I bring this to your attention not to warn you of the minor cuts and stubbed toes my wife and kids suffer each day at the hands of these landmines, but because I was recently speared by one of these toys, and spent the longest ten seconds of my life with the bayonet of some armed action figure up my ass.

the helmet cop

#46

My son is a bit of a helmet cop. We ride around on our bikes and he yells at people for not wearing a helmet. He even yells at me and his mom if we start riding without fully strapping our helmets to our heads. Even though my little pea-head is too small for my body, and my choice of helmets are one's that are too big and look like a fruit bowl on my skull, or the one's that fit but have pictures of Elmo or Dora on them, I like to set a good example for my son. In fact as ridiculous as they look on my shrunken head, I've always worn a helmet, even before my son was born.

We've always preached the importance of wearing a helmet to him. Whether it was his first tricycle, scooter or skateboard, he always had to wear a helmet. In fact as a baby he was always smashing his head into table legs and the corners of cabinets so I got him a helmet just to crawl around the house in. I guess with our deep helmet obsession, we somehow drove the point home a little too hard. But I don't think that's necessarily a bad thing considering where we live. Every year a couple of locals are run down on their bikes by tourists in their cars, oblivious to everyone and everything except the allusive free parking spot near the beach.

A couple of weeks before my son was to have begun school, his teacher was killed on her bicycle when a truck bumped into her at a four way stop. Just a little confusion as to who had the right of way, a tiny tap of a truck's bumper, and the lack of a helmet did her in.

My son got pretty righteous after that and made it his mission to convert all bare heads to hard plastic clad ones. He was sometimes over the top and I braced for some backlash. I expected the local teens to goof on him, or the soccer moms to roll their eyes. But the only feedback he received was from an old ex-hippie surfer dude, who looked like he spent too many nights in the pubs and too many mornings sleeping it off on a bench. His gray speckled, dry and brittle longish mop of hair, flapped in the breeze like straw as he peddled past us.

My son called out to him as he did to anyone else who wasn't wearing protective gear, "Wear a helmet!" Without pause, the ex-hippie surfer dude with a red bulbous nose and a head of hair celebrating its freedom called back, "Fuck Off!"

My son still points out to me kids who are skating or biking without the proper cranial protection, and will call out in almost a whisper, "Wear a helmet." But he's moved on to other causes and can only occasionally muster up the passion to helmet the world.

ALEX GOETCHIUS

Crumpled notes

47

I used to always find the notes that I left in my son's lunchbox, crumpled underneath his seat in the car. I guess he fished them out of his lunch when I wasn't looking. I'm sure he did this to spare himself the embarrassment of having to read what these notes might have said, with his classmates hovering over his shoulder. This is understandable, since sometimes my notes were a little off color. But usually the notes just sent him love and wished him well.

Recently, while looking under the seat for my dropped keys and spare change for the highway tolls, I found a crumpled note that said, "I love you, have a great day!"

I don't bother giving the notes I write to my son anymore, I just write them, crumple them up and throw them under his seat. Now when I find a note while cleaning out my car, I just pretend it was left for me.

sometimes art is shit

48

What is it with kids who don't flush the toilet when they're done taking a crap? Do they really think their poo is so special it should be enshrined there forever? My son must think every shit he takes is a work of art. He must think we'll find them as wonderful as his paintings and sketches, and frame them and hang them on the wall. Or photograph them and send them to art galleries and maybe get him a solo show.

It's bad enough that I stumble upon these little gems on my own, but sometimes he'll trick me into coming into the bathroom with fake cries for help, or pretending he wants me to read to him. When I get in there he's flashing a wicked smile and he makes me look.

Today it was after the dean of admissions at a prestigious and progressive private elementary school called my wife about our son attending in the fall. My son answered the phone "with a piece of poo still hanging from my ass." He told the dean that "Mom is in the pool with my sister". She asked my son "Why aren't you out there with them?" and he told her "I'm on the toilet, wiping."

Despite the lousy traffic I drove home from work in, I was in a pretty decent mood. I just smiled at my son's version of the phone call, while my wife shook her head partly with embarrassment, and partly to signal me that my son was taking liberties with the truth. The whole thing amused me.

Until I walked into the bathroom to relieve myself of the worst part of a two hour commute, and saw my son's latest work. It was another masterpiece of corn and carrots, turkey burgers, organic blue chips and a strawberry popsicle. I took a picture and then flushed.

I added the photo to his portfolio in the event that this new school's art classes are more liberal than his last.

rain Dance

49

My daughter was running around in a party dress just before bedtime. My son was spinning out of control like his hair was on fire. My kids were doing their "over tired" rain dance on one of the down comforters. They wrestled a little and then my son stretched out across the bed while his sister did her best to maneuver around this human speed bump. She twirled like a top, stumbled over him and giggled like a lunatic. He in turn hugged and kissed her each time she fell.

But at some point my daughter positioned herself over my son and gave him a perfect view of her diaper less ass. "Hey Dad, she took her diaper off!!!" My son laughed hysterically at her bare butt hovering above him, just as my daughter let loose and pissed on his head. The rain dance opened up the sky and let the rain fall on my son.

She must have thought his hair was really on fire.

Getting Kicked Out of Art Class

50

Only in a public school could an art teacher, responsible for helping children creatively express themselves, be so stiff, stoic and inflexible. My son took a week long summer camp art program in our town's public school. It's a school that we heard great things about and subsequently moved here for that school when he was born. My son spent a total of two months there before transferring to a more tolerant and nurturing private school. But the summer camps there are only twenty-five bucks a week, so we figured we'd give it a try.

After the first day of art class my son was asked to leave. The teacher recognized that what he had painted was different and interesting, and that watching him paint was a bit of a thrill. But she must have been beaten down by the public school system, or maybe she was hiding in the middle of it so she could keep her job. Either way, she wasn't about to make waves or let my son continue to do it for her, so she tossed him out of the class.

During the class, my son was taking handfuls of paint and launching them like hand grenades at his painting. He exploded blue and yellow bombs, and sprayed rainbows like machine gun fire against a defenseless white canvas. That's not to say that the canvas didn't put up a good fight, but teachers and canvas alike, eventually wilt against the kamikaze energy he has.

My son throws himself into everything. And so, long before his painting was close to being finished, he and the walls and floors were covered with no less paint than the canvas. My son got caught up in the moment and spun out of control. He crashed into the canvas, spilling everywhere hundreds of vibrant splatters and swirls.

So, you can see the canvas never had a chance against the force of my son in creative ecstasy, and neither did his teacher. I think the system wore her down and instead of sitting back and admiring his fire burning, and possibly feeding it twigs and branches, she poured cold water over it instead. That's probably why it took so long for the painting to dry.

And in case you're wondering, after my son's assault of multi-colored bombs and missiles, instead of dying, the canvas was brought to life.

Plug and Play Children

51

Wouldn't it be nice if kids were plug and play? Turn them on and follow the online instructions. But no, instead we need a team of IT guys to trouble shoot the installation, the upgrades and the operating system when it becomes infected with viruses.

They walk you through step by step procedures. "Are his lights green or red? Are you sure he's turned on? What does the error message say?" Fuck, he's only four I don't know what turns him on!!! And the error message says, " I NEED A COUPLE OF COCKTAILS!!!" The IT guy reminds me "When all else fails, give him a full reboot." So I read him a bed time story even though the sun's still out. I kiss him on his head and go suck down a couple of scotch and waters. Then I wait for the morning and hope the reboot makes everything nice again.

Washing Diapers

#52

Shouldn't there be some kind of alarm with flashing lights and wailing sirens when you're about to wash a diaper!?!?!

Now I've got a washer and wet pile of clothes filled with what looks like tiny jellyfish that collectively absorb baby piss. It's beginning to feel like I'll be in diapers before my daughter is out of them.

ALEX GOETCHIUS

my son, the comedian

53

My son is a standup comedian and performance artist who thrills the crowd on the playground, but not so much his audience of one in the principal's office at school.

The teacher in his class asks "Does anyone know what a prism is?" With his head on his desk, my eight year old son mutters under his breath but loud enough for all to hear, "It's where they put bad people."

My son at times is the funniest person I know. His humor is so adult that I forget he's just a little boy, and in some ways, just a baby. His wit is sharp and boarders on highbrow, but he's just as apt to sing Christmas carols out of his ass, or throw himself into a large building of Legos to make his sister laugh. His two year old sister, who thinks it's funny to stick both index fingers up her nose even when there's no green nuggets to mine, is my son's biggest supporter. My wife and I are also big supporters of his comic genius even if we have to hide our support behind hands that muffle our laughter. Grownups just aren't supposed to laugh at this stuff.

My son performs daily at the library, the local coffee shop and his 2nd grade classroom. His naked performance at the coffee shop at the age of four, excited a crowd of giddy teenage girls who squealed with glee when he shook his little bubble butt, like they were watching Elvis or the Beatles. His library performances have been met with mixed reviews. The younger crowd of toddlers to teens can really relate to the message in his routine, but the librarians with their hair pulled back so tight that it's impossible for them to crack a real smile, voice their disapproval with emphatic bursts of "SHHHHHHHHH!!"

At school, the audience is a tough crowd. The teachers and students alike don't understand his act, and his material, which is thinly disguised barbs at them, spreads its mighty wings and soars right over most of their heads. The ones who do get it, march him right down to the office, and the show ends abruptly without a single curtain call.

When it comes to conventional learning my son has two strikes against him right from the start. He's way brighter than the material, and in some cases, smarter than the teachers. I know this might sound like biased boasting, but believe me having a child this smart is equal amounts of blessing and curse.

In addition to his intellect he just can't sit still and so while his mind races out of control, his body stumbles and dances through walls. It's like someone over-wound his little tin toy body and brain. After years of dealing with this wicked combination, the best advice we have to give him is "If you're going to be bored in class, try not to do it so loudly." We tell him when his mind is under-stimulated, or his body is out of control, "if you feel like this at school, go to the bathroom and do a bunch of jumping jacks, and sweat it out of your system, but for god's sake, wash your hands when you're done in there. There's baby piss and shit all over everything, and the last thing I need is for you to be touching me with nasty dirty fingers!"

My son walks through the bathroom door and hears the teacher ask, "Does anyone know what symmetry is?"

My son dries his hands with a brown paper towel and then tosses it in the trash.

"It's where they put dead people," he says as he walks back to his seat.

the Dandelion Garden

54

My son loves to pull the dandelion stems from our yard and from the neighbor's, and blow the white fluffy seeds into the air. I tell him to make a wish as the seeds land on the ground inside our white picket fence. And because most of his wishes come true we have a dandelion garden growing in our front yard. The dandelions look like a thousand small suns floating in a bright green sky.

I'm of the opinion that if you have a perfect lawn you either have way too much time on your hands and not enough hobbies, or you have a really good gardener. I personally can't afford a really good gardener or lawn care guy, and I'm here writing rather than planting seeds and killing weeds, so I instead have a lush collection of dandelions poking their heads through the grass.

Except for the bare patches of dirt from my pulling up by the roots, sprawling legs of crabgrass, to me my lawn is perfect. I love my dandelions so much because they grow all by themselves no matter how much or little care I give them. And when my kids stomp on them or I cut their heads off with the lawn mower, they happily grow back two fold, as if that's all the loving they need.

I've thought about letting them grow as high as sunflowers grow, but that might upset the neighbors who freak out when their lawn sports even a single weed. But as long as I keep seeing pictures of my kids rolling around in our dandelion garden, playing together and laughing, the thousands of small suns can stay and shine brightly beside a couple of patches of dirt and a handful of blades of grass.

Skid Marks Blowing in the Breeze

#55

My son accidentally wore two pair of underpants to school yesterday, a fact he didn't discover until gym class. Now there have been times where we've pulled up to his school fifteen miles away, and he's realized he's forgotten to put underwear on at all. On those occasions I've had to take him back home to put on a pair, and be a half hour late, rather than go bareback and be on time. Two pairs at once however is new territory for my son, but it's an honest mistake, he was in a rush and half asleep when he pulled a pair of clean underwear over the ones he wore to bed.

During gym, he wound up sneaking out and take off the dirty pair. He waved it around the class for a few minutes before he was told to put them away. When my wife came to pick up my son from school, he handed her the pair to hold and told her what had happened. With one ear on my son's story, and then forgetting she was still holding them in her hand, she waved goodbye to all the teachers and parents with my son's skid marks blowing in the breeze.

the monsters we were to each other

56

When I was a kid my mom used to call me a monster. Because of this I sometimes lived under my bed. I'd bring my toys and meals under there and pretend it was my cave. I imagined the toys were from villages that I plundered and my meals were the small pets of the families who lived in the village. To make sure that the rest of my family would be safe from me, I taped a handmade sign to the edge of the bed that said "Beware of Monster." Looking back, I'm sure I must have done something terribly wrong, or forgotten to do something really important, because you have to piss someone off pretty bad for them to make you feel so awful.

But I'm beginning to remember now, my mother hugging me and kissing my head to take the sting away from the names she called me. I remember feeling her guilt and grief in those hugs. I'm hoping now that I've begun to embrace the way my parents raised me, despite all their flaws in doing so, my kids will be able to appreciate at some point in their lives, my own attempts at raising them.

For all the terrible names I call my son while battling the monster in him, I pray to whatever power greater than me that will listen, that all my hugs and kisses will comfort him more than my poisoned words have burned. I hope it doesn't take him half his life (like it took me), to realize the names we say are misguided lies in passing fits of rage, while the love comes from a place that lives forever.

no Presents this year

57

I had to return my son's birthday presents today so I could buy groceries. We bought them a few weeks early and snuck them into a closet without him seeing. I had to sneak them back out and into my car without my son catching on a second time. That's not an easy task given that he hears everything that goes on in the house. He hears everything except for the requests to clean his room, or get ready for school. Those things are ignored with a unique brand of selective deafness.

Star Wars 3: The Clone Wars, SpongeBob Drawn to Life for DS, Lego Alien Conquest kit and some pretty sweet SpongeBob wrapping paper all had to go back so my debit card was a little thicker than paper thin. I've had to get creatively diabolical over the years just to pay the bills, but having to return my kids birthday presents is a new low even for me.

The bills that get paid with the first check of the month don't leave much wiggle room for anything but the necessities. But it's rare when I find myself at a Toys R Us and with the time to stop in, so I figured I'd wing it and try and balance the budget after the fact. I guess it's even rarer when I have enough change in my pockets and cash in the bank to actually buy something once I'm there and inside the store.

So for now the toys sit back on their shelves until the end of the week, but at least I have a spare $98 for groceries. And so it goes in the 21st century where the middle class are the nouveau poor, and we struggle to find ways to spoil our children on a shoe-string budget.

sent to the office

58

There's a wing of the office in the school my son goes to that's named after him. With all the money we've given that school, and for the amount of time he spends in the office, a wing really should be named in his honor. But in actuality it's not so much a wing as a corner. At the very least, his chair in there should have a little gold plaque with his name engraved in it. But I bet he winds up carving his name into it with a pencil anyway, if he spends anymore time in there.

The chair faces the corner of two walls but he sits backwards in it with his legs poking through the curved openings in the backrest. He sits that way when the Principal leaves the room, and stares out the windows at the farm animals to the left, kids in the playground to the right, and the highway straight ahead. I know he'd rather be feeding his classmates carrots from his hand, or playing soccer with the Llama and the goats. But what his imagination runs wild with instead is the highway straight ahead. He imagines crawling out the window and darting between the cars in the parking lot, before making his getaway on a skateboard or bicycle he's hidden in the bushes days before.

He's in there because he wore his pencil box as a hat. And if I know my son, he danced, sang or told an off color joke to accompany the visual performance. That was the final straw for his teacher, in a day filled with his tiny acts of defiance. "GET OUT!!!" she screamed as he slithered down the stairs, and cart wheeled his way through the doors of the principal's office.

Once there he reached into a glass bowl filled with individually wrapped hard candy. "Can I have a piece?" he asked just before he stuffed a watermelon jolly rancher in his mouth. "No!" Mr. Principal Man would say incredulously. "You're in the office! You don't get candy!" Of course as far as I'm concerned, and I believe my son will agree, the person who needs candy most is the one who's been sent to the office.

As the Principal's lecture echoes off in the distance my son stares at 4' by 6' painting hanging on the wall. "Do you know the artist who painted this?" my son asks, interrupting Mr. Principal Man's beautiful speech. And just like that the lecture is lost to a more lofty conversation about art and his connection to the artist.

The Principal revels in the telling of the story and exaggerates some details about his relationship with artist. But who'll ever know. Certainly not my son who has now slipped past the self-consumed Mr. Principal Man, through the front door and into the getaway car with me as its driver.

I try to imagine each circumstance that gets my son sent to the office so I can understand exactly how he feels while he's there. Because when I was his age I was terrified of the office and the principal Mr. Evans. The only time I was ever sent to the office, I nearly shriveled up and died. I escaped to see another day but poor Eddie Scablon got sent to the office and never came back. I wilted under the bright interrogating lights of the office that my son seems to thrive on.

Mr. Evans would pick up lunch tables and slam them to the ground to silence 200 screaming kids. Plates of food would fly into the air, and on unsuspecting kids. The last second warnings of whispered screams came too late. "Evans! It's Evans!! Run!!! It's Mr. Evans!!!"

Even after we graduated from school his ominous presence was still felt whenever my friends and I would see a cop hiding in the weeds or racing past us with lights flashing. "Evans!" we'd tell each other just on case someone hadn't noticed.

I wonder how my son would have fared under the iron fist of Mr. Evans?

I see the fear in my son's eyes on the rare occasions my rage takes control. Rage is an effective weapon I rarely ever use, and it's always a last resort. But Mr. Evans would have used it as a first, second and third resort just to make a point. There'd be no discussions of art and my son would feel the worst of his wrath if he grabbed a piece of candy.

For my son's sake I hope he would cave in at that point, and realize there was no talking his way out of this mess. I want my son to challenge authority. I want him to look at life and yell to the heavens "WHY?" I want him to learn to stand up for himself and anyone else who might be getting a bum rap. But I also want him to know when the fight is better left not fought. Sometimes you just have to take your punishment like a man and learn from the lesson's pain.

the Dishwasher from hell

59

My dishwasher caught on fire last night, and I have mixed feelings about it. Smoke billowed out from it and I raced into the basement to flip the switch in the fuse box, before it took down the rest of the house. When I went back upstairs and tried to disconnect the wires from the machine, a jolt of current ran through me, threw me backwards against the wall in the back of the pantry, where a few pots and pans fell and conked me on the head. Obviously I had flipped the wrong switch.

From as far back as I can remember that dishwasher never worked right. It didn't clean as much as it rinsed and dried. If you put dirty dishes in the machine that had even a little bit of sauce on them, the dishes would come out feeling freshly baked, but the sauce would still remain.

In the beginning, at least the parts of the dirty dishes not caked with food would be shiny and squeaky clean to the touch. But even then the oatmeal at the bottom of a breakfast bowl, and the last sip of coffee at the bottom of a tea cup, felt like they were part of the ceramic, like they'd been baked into each piece. By the end, you could put perfectly clean dishes in the dishwasher and they would come out dirty.

I found myself at other people's houses watching with envy as their dirty dishes magically came out of their machines clean. I began frequenting salad bars just to stand in line and hold a warm smooth plate against my face. I'd caress the plate with my fingers, and finding not a single imperfection, I'd brush it against my cheek. All you can eat? Why bother. The warm, smooth plate against my face was worth the price of admission alone.

My wife has no interest in scrubbing dishes before loading them into the machine because for a while that's what it took to make them clean. She has a real hard time looking at food that's been handled and chewed, or left to sit out for more than a few minutes. She always wonders how anyone could ever be a waiter or a busboy and have to touch other people's unwanted and decaying meals. So, it doesn't seem to bother her much if a few cups and saucers come out of the cupboard with food or drink still in them. I guess she figures that the "leftovers", while still visible, have at least been through a wash cycle.

Already chewed and nearly eaten, caked on, baked on, buffed and polished food isn't what I want to see when

I'm about to pour my morning coffee or butter my morning toast. So I've taken it upon myself to make doing the dishes one of my chores. If you want something done right you have to do it yourself, or hire a pro to do it for you. Of course I barely have enough money to pay for dish detergent so hiring a pro is not happening.

While we had this machine that barely worked, at least we knew the routine, as cumbersome as it was, to make dishes clean. But now it doesn't work at all, and the house smells like fried electrical components. But worse than that, my empty wallet looks up at me incredulously and shrugs its shoulders, because it has no more answers than I do.

Children are a wise investment

60

A friend of mine and I were comparing balance sheets trying to see who has "invested" more money in their kids. He is helping raise two young adults who he and his lovely girlfriend inherited from the boys' father. His "new" kids have lived a tumultuous life with a closet full of baggage, and the expense of trying to undo what other less caring people have done, is considerable. I on the other hand have raised my kids from the moment they were sperm swimming upstream, fighting an against-all-odds battle. Hopefully, by the time they are young adults themselves, there won't be too great of an expense trying to undo our own parenting.

It's really a pointless task comparing one set of parents' balance sheets with another. But I believe keeping track of the expenses your children have demanded is a good thing. It's nice to have a little factual ammunition when they're acting particularly badly, and you threaten to sell them off to the highest bidder.

So whether you try and fix a couple of older kids who someone else broke, or you try and fix a couple of newborns you broke all by yourself, the expense of the undertaking is way more than anyone can plan for. Especially when you consider the interest that debt will accrue, over the twenty or thirty years it will take your kids to find a well-paying job, and start to pay it off.

I love my kids and I doubt I'd ever really make them pay me back. So rather than a loan, I like to consider the money spent on private schools, art classes, Lego construction kits, animation workshops and healthy raw organic snacks, an investment.

I know one day I'll be old and over ripe like a brown banana. When the fruit flies finally come and circle above me, my only wish will be that because of the money I've invested in them, my kids will be able to afford to have someone else change my diapers, instead of having to do it themselves.

Ugh, I'm REALLY looking forward to that part of my life! Maybe it would be cheaper to invest in a well-constructed shovel they can crack my skull with, and then dig a hole to dump me in.

time to Buy another clock

61

My wife took my daughter and son to a party yesterday afternoon while I stayed home and worked on the house. After building a Barbie play land for my daughter, my son went downstairs to make friends with the TV. My wife told him he only had until 4 o'clock and then they had to leave.

A little while later another party guest came upstairs and announced, "The kid down stairs changed the time on the clock." My son had drawn numbers on white paper, cut them out and taped them over the existing numbers on the digital clock so that it said 3:65 PM. My wife walked downstairs where my son was being hypnotized by a Sponge Bob marathon. My wife snapped him from his glazed over haze and told him "there's no such time as 3:65." "Yeah there is," my son said, "It's 5 minutes to 4. It's always going to be 5 minutes to 4 here."

I have to give him credit for trying to make time stand still long enough to fully enjoy every last bit of Sponge Bob's antics. But I think it's time my son and I work on his lessons on telling time before he permanently alters the relationship between time and space forever. Either that or it's time to get a new clock, and not one from the surrealist's store.

War Called Due to Bladder

62

Last winter was particularly cold and snowy, and my son and I tried our best to ignore the freezing winds and impossible to navigate snowdrifts, by sledding and building snow men. One morning, when the sun finally reached its arms through the gray canopy of clouds, we went out into the yard to build a snowman.

As I was rolling a small ball of snow into a bigger one for the snowman's body, my son was pelting me with rocks of ice. Not snow balls that he had packed with his hands, but ice balls that had been packed by nature or plows from the night before. The elements had conspired against me by freezing clumps of loose snow into weapons, and my son had taken full advantage of it.

I occasionally fired back more conventional snowballs, as I continued to build the snowman's body. We pretended that we were two armies fighting. We lobbed snowy artillery across the walkway that divided the two sides of the front yard. The walkway served as a frozen river that separated his army from mine.

Most if his snowballs exploded near, but not on me, and I used the powdered shrapnel to roll my snowman's midsection. We pretended the snowman was going to be a giant robot that would protect my army from his, and his mission was to destroy my robot snowman and conquer my side of the river.

After playing like this for about an hour, my son ran behind a bush to pee. I could have destroyed his army while he tried to spell his name in the snow, but instead I quietly built my peace-keeping snowbot.

The war eventually ended not because the two sides had reached some kind of peace accord, but because my son had a bit of difficulty navigating the buttons on his snow pants and wound up pissing on himself. It was just as well, he never really got any good snowball shots at me from a distance and when he moved in close, I forced him back with a few snowballs I had stockpiled.

As we walked in the house and the last of the pee dripped from the bottom of his pants cuff, I asked him, "How are you going to conquer anyone's pretend army if you can't throw or even pee straight?"

Wearing Baby Snot for Clothes

63

When both of my kids were babies, my shoulders were always covered in spit-up and my sleeves were always covered in snot. There were times when we'd be out and I'd find myself without any tissues, napkins or baby wipes. I guess that makes me a suspect parent for teaching my children to use their sleeves to wipe their nose and mouth. But in my defense I only resorted to using my sleeves when I couldn't convince strangers to let me use theirs.

ALEX GOETCHIUS

wtf?

64

When my son was in preschool he was building a structure made from blocks in class one day, and some girl came along and knocked it over. My son held his arms out with palms up, and shoulders shrugged and said "What the fuck is that!?" The teacher was stunned and immediately met us at the door when we came to pick him up. I told her I'd never heard him say that before and that he must have picked it up from someone in school. She stared at me in disbelief and scolded me with an accusing tone. I barked back at her, "What the fuck kind of school are you running here!?"

ALEX GOETCHIUS

my Dad Shaved his Back

65

Just the other day my son was on the phone with his friend when he went into the bathroom to take a piss. He lifted the toilet seat and yelled into the phone, "Holy crap my dad shaved his back into the toilet."

That's not exactly true. It wasn't my back, it was my head but what's the difference? Actually I'll tell you what the difference is, my back has way more hair on it than my head. Yeah, I know what you're thinking, "That's so fucking sexy!"

I feel fortunate that having more hair on my back, my ass, my feet, my ears, my stomach and my palms, than anywhere on my head, is as bad as it gets for me. A recent full body scan even showed hair on my spleen. It also showed where my spare keys were, but that's another story.

The gods must have been in one funny mood when they put me together, and so I'm thankful this is the worst they did to me. The gods must have been bored with building perfection in the form of saints, scientists and super models that day, and spent the better part of it making freaks for the circus instead.

The freaks rolled down the assembly line one by one that day. The dog faced boy and a family of albinos were just in front of me, a woman with Tourette's and a man with his twin growing from his neck, stood right behind. And in the middle of them all was me the human fur ball standing in my shoes. The gods sure had a good laugh at our expense that day.

Maybe if I had spent more time believing in them when I was younger, the gods wouldn't have chosen me to fuck with. I had long flowing locks that hung down to the middle of my back then. Now I have the long flowing locks growing out of my back. But back then, the hair on my head was lush and soft and fun to run barefoot through, and I only had a small patch of hair on my chest and a soft wisp of hair on my stomach.

But slowly over time the hair on my head fell out in patches that left me looking like a middle aged hippy trying to hold on to the last of his freak flag. But I think, by the gods' design, the clumps of hair that fell off in the shower planted little seedlings on my back and shoulders on their way down the drain.

My son likes to run his hands through the hair on my chest that's now as white as Santa's beard or freshly fallen snow. He marvels at how much fur there is and laughs at how his fingers disappear in it. He giggles at me when he sees me naked coming out of the shower looking like a shaggy dog caught out in the rain, or when he tries to pull an eyebrow hair that's grown too long, out of its socket.

Yeah I shave my head with a beard trimmer because it grows in uneven, lopsided and only on parts of my head. I throw the clippings into the toilet bowl because it's easier than picking them up from the floor or trying to rinse them down the drain. It pains me to throw away something I have so little of to spare. But the hair on the rest of my body grows like wild flowers in a fertile field that would only grow thicker with each trimming.

Underneath the giggles I see the far off look of concern in my son's eyes that one day he'll be looking like a drowned rat in the shower, and will have to shave his back with a lawn mower. Yeah, it's not so funny now, is it little man?

Christmas Comes early

66

This Christmas Eve, we spent the entire day telling my son that Christmas was two days away. Everywhere we went we had to correct people when they asked my son if he was excited about tomorrow morning. At one store in the small Christmas village of Smithville a self-proclaimed "Christmas celebrating Jew" asked my son if he'd been good all year, and told him she hoped my son got everything he asked for tomorrow morning. I had to tell him she was confused about when Christmas was, probably because she spent her whole life celebrating Hanukkah. We did this so that my son wouldn't lay awake all night waiting for Christmas. And so while his best friends parents had to wake up with their son at 3:45 am to open presents, my family got to sleep in late.

ALEX GOETCHIUS

sleeping is Believing

#67

Last night my daughter woke up and for the first time instead of crying out for her mom, she reached out to me. It caught me off guard because she's always latched on to her mother's boob to put herself back to sleep. So at first I thought I was hallucinating.

Babies don't have the decency to let you sleep for more than a couple of minutes at a time when they're newborn, and more than a couple of hours at a time after a they're a few months old. The constant state of nodding off only to be woken by a blood curdling scream, is the kind of torture Hell does envy. The longer babies nurse, the longer it can take them to fall asleep on their own and end their reign of terror.

I can't provide the suckling sensation and the milk, but I can offer a big barreled chest for my daughter to lay her head down on, and a warm and cozy body to curl up against. I can give her the tips of my fingers that gently brush her hair out of her eyes, and the hush from my breathing that lulls her to sleep.

These sleepless nights, which I know will eventually end, are grueling. The nightly event can really take its toll on the body and the mind. But when I look down and see her curled up next to me I can barely contain the love I feel for her, and the last thing I want to do is sleep.

my son is an endless stream of energy

#68

My son is an endless stream of energy the moment the sun pushes open his eyes and he bounces out of bed, until he instantly loses his steam and crashes back in it at night. He doesn't fall asleep so much as he speeds head on into it. Once he rises, he is a twirling top spinning his way from room to room, not like a graceful whirling dervish but more like an epileptic bull in a china shop chasing its tail.

Things smash against the wall and explode on the floor as he moves past them. His perpetual motion is hypnotizing and makes him appear to any onlooker as a blur, until his presence is nearly imperceptible. After a while the only way you know he's been in the same room as you, is the wreckage of the no longer valuables, scattered around the room.

My son is like this for only some of the day, so there's always a little time to rebuild the ruins. As I assess the damage of his latest tornado, and pick up the pieces left in his wake, I think to myself "give me just a bit of that energy, just enough to clean up this mess."

fishinG LeGOs from the trash

69

I spent my morning fishing through the garbage cans at the local coffee shop, in search of red Lego legs that I accidentally tossed out. I took my kids there for lunch, and together we shared a toasted bagel, two yogurts and a smoothie, in between the bursts of energy that catapulted my kids around the coffee shop like it was a jungle gym.

Somehow in the middle of wiping yogurt from my daughter's mouth, wiping smoothie from my son's pants, and wiping sweat from my brow, I amassed a large collection of used and soggy paper napkins in all four of my pockets.

Unfortunately, the red Lego legs that we just got in the mail were also wrapped inside a paper towel and tucked inside a pocket with them.

It wasn't until long after I emptied my pockets into a couple of different garbage cans that my son asked me for his Lego legs. That's when and why I found myself elbows deep in the mixed together leftovers of hundreds of strangers. Lipstick stained paper cups stuffed with half eaten muffins and the backwash of some oozing cream and sugar coffee concoction. The vile stench and the burden my eyes and fingers had to bear were enough to make me lose my lunch. I coughed out the last swill of my own bagel and coffee and spit it in the bottom of the can.

People were actually throwing shit into the trash as I was rifling through it!!! Paper cups crashed against the bottom of the can and sprayed cold coffee on my arms.

One dirty diaper was gently placed in the can I was excavating, while other cans sat idle and empty. It's a good thing my son is cute, otherwise I wouldn't put up with such shit. He knows how much I love him and that's all that matters. Compared to that, pride and dignity are almost pointless.

After digging through the muck and mire, and pouring one garbage can's contents into another, I never found the red Lego legs. I did however find the lunch I lost just a few minutes before.

imaGinary frienDs

#70

My son has always had imaginary friends. They've kept him company when there were no real friends to be had. They've come in all shapes and sizes. But mostly anything small has always been his friend; a piece of left over toast that no one wanted, or the smallest cloud in the sky. These little things he'd tell his secrets to, would eventually break his heart. The hardened piece of toast he'd grown so close to, was crushed beneath his foot, and the small puffy cloud was swallowed up by the bigger ones, as they moved across the sky.

My son's best imaginary friends have been a talking Po doll from the Teletubbies, a Max pillow from Max and

Ruby, and Wicket, a stuffed Ewok. These "stuffies" traveled the world with us surviving the hustle and bustle of Lisbon and Amsterdam airports, and the sun and surf of the Bahamas. They've been out to dinner with us, and catered to by bewildered servers. They've shared well-visits at the doctor's office with my son, and were stained with the free lollypops the receptionist handed out. They've been peed on and puked on and have had a runny nose or two use them as a hanky. But always after a fun tumble in the washing machine and dryer, they're nearly good as new, and clean enough to cuddle.

My son's imaginary friends were always loyal and always true, and stood by his side while most kids his age struggled to understand him. My son would defend his make believe pals from the skeptics who disbelieved. Together they were inseparable and would conquer the world, and their friendship would last forever.

But as soon as my wife got pregnant Max, Po and Wicket found their way first on the shelves inside the closet, and then eventually mixed in with all the other "stuffies" who never meant as much to my son. My son waited all his life for his sister and now that she was here there just wasn't enough room in his heart for his pretend friends.

My son fell in love with his sister from the moment he first saw her, and now he walks past his old friends peering out from the toy chest without even giving them a passing glance. If you ask him how come he never spends any time anymore with Wicket, Max and Po, he gets a little sad and hides his eyes and cries. Then he runs over to his little baby sister and hugs her like she's made of stuffing.

We still have all of my son's imaginary friends. They never really go away. They just wait around like no other loyal friend you've ever had can, until you need them.

ABOUT THE AUTHOR

Alex Goetchius never wanted children. He was doing just fine without them. But a funny thing happened on the way to becoming an accidental dad. He fell in love with his kids.

In other versions of this life Alex has been a musician, playing in clubs in New York City, and a collector of Lowbrow art and supporter of the pop surrealism art movement. But this present version of his life, writing and raising kids, seems to suit him best.

Alex lives with his wife and two children in a small beach town halfway between New York and Philly, where you'll find him at the local pub sipping wine and watching baseball, and quietly writing and giggling to himself.

www.ingramcontent.com/pod-product-compliance
Lightning Source LLC
LaVergne TN
LVHW051830080426
835512LV00018B/2804